DEAR WORLD

Jeff Latham

BEYOND THE GROVE PUBLISHING

DEAR WORLD
Copyright © Jeff Latham 2021

All Rights Reserved

No part of this book may be reproduced in any form,
by photocopying or by any electronic or mechanical means,
Including information storage or retrieval systems,
without permission in writing from both the copyright
owner and the publisher of this book.

ISBN 978-1-5272-9106-5

First Published 2021
Beyond The Grove Publishing

Earth image provided by freepngimg.com

Printed and bound in Great Britain by
www.print2demand.co.uk

DEAR WORLD

To Stu and Josie my friends in the grove of druids

Jeff Latham

For Laura, Ben, James and Zoe.

This book is also dedicated to all those who work for a better world, often silently and unheralded. Those who in their prayers, meditations, actions, healing and being, make a real difference, though they may themselves doubt it. It is my hope that these words will encourage you in the belief that your connections are real and true and you really are making a difference.

Dear World

Introduction

Although for as long as I can remember I have considered myself to be spiritually connected and striving to understand and make positive use of that connection, I have struggled to find a means of communicating that which I seem to know. It was with that in mind and some urging from within that I decided at the end of 2019 to undertake regular short meditations and writing down the words that came to me in consequence of them. I had meditated sporadically for over twenty years, but this had of late become less frequent. So, I decided to commit to at least a fifteen-minute meditation every day and writing down what came through that experience. This began on 30th December, 2019 and I made myself a commitment to continue this practice through the whole of 2020. The meditations grew to becoming nearer an hour in length, but the fifteen-minute promise was successful in initiating the impulse.

Of course, when I began this undertaking, I had no idea what would unfold during the year, but there were some clues in the meditations given to me. This completed year of writings stands as a collection of spiritually inspired words that I would humbly suggest contains some wisdom of merit, hopefully relevant to many readers. It also stands as a social and spiritual record of a unique year as it happened.

The reader may find it useful to follow the writings chronologically to feel the underlying currents that were at play. Alternatively, I would suggest that the book would also be of benefit to dip in and out of as a daily inspiration or to be used in an oracular fashion. There is space under each day's writings for your own reflections if that feels appropriate to you.

Dear World

Introduction

I apologise if anyone finds any content upsetting or contradictory to their beliefs, but my intention was to deter my critical mind and be true in accepting what words or impulse I was given. Everything of course will be subject to the limitations, or otherwise, of my own being and ability to accept and convey the wisdom given. It is my sincere hope that these words give comfort and understanding to you all in these continually changing times.

J.L. January 2021

Dear World

2019

30 December

So here we are, another year ending and another about to begin, a new decade indeed. How silently the precious gift is given. Yet how do we use it, the gift of time and space. Yes, it may be an illusion in astral terms, but in our hearts and minds and earthly bodies it is very real indeed.

'Is it ok just to be?' you say. Yes of course, for in being and holding space you are of service, but how often do you just be? You *do* even when you do nothing. Grace and poise may seem of the past, but they can conjure a state of being that encourages calm and considered action. To be or not to be, that is the question.

Dear World

31 December

Let us talk about love. You feel it in the heart and then throughout the body. This is our natural state, so why does it seem so denied. Beliefs have changed and confused the simplicity of our natural capacity to give and receive love. We are told that there are times and situations when it is wrong for us to love or act on love. That may be so regarding certain intimacies of love, but the feeling of love with another and the desire to share that love is in itself a natural one. Sometimes when we deny nature we deny ourselves and in denying ourselves we deny others.

Dear World

2020

1st January

A new year has started, another number to explore. It is funny how it already feels different. A capsule of time, a circle of existence. Who are they that think they know which way our lives will go? The wind blows one way then another. The minds of men and gods flutter and blow according to their whims.

Dear World

2nd January

So, what of pain? What does it tell us? Something hurts on the inside coming out, or on the outside going in. Our body feels it, we want it to go, but first ask what is its message?

Do our habits and actions need to change? Do we need to acknowledge some long forgotten hurt that is coming into consciousness? Or maybe body and mind are out of line, the walk we walk does not match the talk we talk.

Dear World

3rd January

Dreams and plans add colour to our lives. There is no harm in looking forward with hope and joy. Sometimes though, life is what happens when we are aiming for our dreams. At times what may feel a hindrance or irritation on your journey, may be a stepping-stone, a skill or knowledge gathered to help you on your way.

Dear World

4th January

Is hope futile? Is it a foolish wish for things to be better? No, hope is valid, because it is a vibration of optimism that encourages participation in life. Hope strives for the certainty of faith, but has a humility that encourages and enhances the possibility of fulfilment and sometimes hope is all we have.

Dear World

5th January

Exercise in moderation according to your need and ability is a wonderful thing. Being active outdoors and in nature is uplifting for your soul and ourselves. It raises your spirit and makes it easier for us to help you receive positive thoughts and feelings. There is a time to rest and a time to play, all in balance. Mother nature is our nature. Being outside reminds body, mind and spirit of this truth.

Dear World

6th January

Healing is a gift bestowed upon a chosen few, though many have the potential. We see what needs to be done and impress that need on you, those that undertake the healing. The art of stilling the mind, listening, feeling and then focusing the forces of love, light and compassion upon the person, creature or situation, takes practice and some dedication. It is always needed.

Dear World

7th January

Children are a blessing. They teach us much in their play and directness. In their smiles and tears lies the story of life. A day in the life of a young child is an emotional roller coaster that some never get off. We help the child to smooth out the ride, to feel and let go. So why not for adults too?

Dear World

8th January

We all encounter crisis in our lives that may be personal, family-related, national or international in nature. How do we respond? We may feel like collapsing under the despair and weight of it, especially when one follows another, but if we look back at our lives we will see that many of these crisis are now behind us. We survived them. As the saying goes they may have made us stronger. We are never powerless when faced with a disturbing situation, even if miles away from us. We can hold it in our thoughts, prayers and meditations, see and feel a positive outcome. This we can all do.

Dear World

9th January

Opportunity comes in many guises as we go through life. Some we take, some we do not. Some we do not realise they were there until they have passed. They are a gift, an answer to a prayer or heartfelt desire. Opportunities occur when paths, conditions and circumstances align. Be thankful that they come along when needed, for your heart then must be true.

Dear World

10th January

Speaking your truth is a desired thing and part of everyone's evolution. It is equally important to listen and hear the truth of others, for this does not invalidate yours. We are all observing life and the universe from a different perspective relative to our journey in this life and the life of our soul. Speaking and listening to the truth of others in a spirit of openness encourages assimilation of ideas into the collective consciousness and aids the development of humanity.

Dear World

11th January

A different kind of love exists here, more flowing, more open. There is no jealousy, for love of one does not negate love for another. We think of someone we love and we are with them. In this way you and we in spirit can connect on earth. This is also your potential concerning earthly existence. It is not as far away as you might think. Bless you all.

Dear World

12th January

Sympathy for others comes when we put ourselves in their shoes and consider what we would feel in that situation. That is an empathetic reaction, which is generally desirable. It is also however, a projection of our beliefs on that situation. They may be feeling relief or even happiness if they are looking at an end to their pain or suffering, or that of a loved one. It pays to be mindful in our caring of others.

Dear World

13th January

Peace in the world and in ourselves is not guaranteed. It comes and goes according to the disturbances in our ether. This varies according to our activities and the alignment or misalignment of the world around us to our ideal. As you know we can work on our inner peace by adopting a state of grace and inner calm. This is easy to do when life is calm, but harder when life is in turmoil. To help in this, hold the vision of single drops of water falling into a still pool and the ripples slowly radiating outwards. In this, peace becomes you.

Dear World

14th January

Fires, floods and destruction are nothing new of course, but their extremes at this time are significant and even the insensitive sense their greater significance. It is true, nature is angry, or thrown out of balance by man's overheating. Sometimes the signs need to be seen to shock and engender change, but there are those among you who have the responsibility to bridge the divide between nature, spirit and man. In raising consciousness and therefore awareness of responsibility, suffering and destruction can be lessened. In this task we are entrusted.

Dear World

15th January

War and fighting, what is it good for? You may think that god or the gods want war, for in your eyes they do not seem to stop it, but in the earth experiment or experience all are given free will. It is true that we try to influence the spiritual development of earth and humanity in certain ways. Sometimes the misunderstanding of this guidance can be a factor in disputes, as can resistance to change or fear of the ways of others. Sometimes in your own lives you have to stand up for injustice, so this is also true on a national or international level. Early genuine diplomacy and honest dialogue can save many a battle.

Dear World

16th January

Let us talk about you and me, guide and master, guide and incarnate soul on earth. Where in lies the separation, if any. It is true, we often communicate by thought and feeling, so sometimes you may wonder what thoughts are your own. You will notice that in communication we can use the "we" of we in spirit, this infers guidance from the spiritual plane, but part of you resides in that sphere also. You could say that the main role of a spiritual guide is to remind you of that, so you can source your own wisdom. If the wisdom of the message rings true, then maybe it does not matter. Although at times we allow the message and thoughts of a clearly separate spiritual identity to come through, in general for heartfelt human communication it is best if the words that come to you are from your own wellspring of use and familiarity.

Dear World

17th January

Families are what make us. Our first impressions can mould a child for life. The cards we are dealt may vary according to our soul's karma and wishes. Before birth, the family situation is chosen by agreement for that which is most likely to give the best circumstances for security, love, life lessons and the playing out of karmic lessons for all involved. Sometimes the family is the foundation for later work in life, or early dynamics are the karmic resolutions. It is important to remember these are not punishments, but the education of the soul through experience and empathy. Nothing is guaranteed in the way a family life plays out. Events may have to be introduced to ensure the development agreed upon before incarnation is given opportunity to happen.

Dear World

18th January

Let us talk about spirit. That which is invisible to most, but its effect is apparent in all things and at all times. You may believe things of spirit are a mystery, but all things are a mystery until they become apparent. The discovery of the nature of spirit is usually an experiential process. This means that through gradual experience and the development of the inner and outer senses, you become aware of cause, effect and sensations that you conclude by default must be generated by spirit. At the same time as you become aware of these effects, you awaken to your own spirit, because this is the part of you that connects to all and reminds you of your limitless potential in that sphere of being. According to the experience of your soul, this can also feel like a remembering, an awakening of that which we already knew deep down inside.

Dear World

19th January

Sadness becomes you at times. We see it and it saddens us too. When the heart is heavy with the water of emotional hurt, it pushes away the joy of life. Sadness comes for many reasons. Sometimes they seem unfathomable to the one suffering. At these times it may come from beyond the personal, at least in part. Misuse of nature and the world's resources and the quickening of change that results, are awakening a grieving for what is being lost. This we understand and can share in. We urge you to focus on the best future world you can imagine and believe in it, for this will not only lift your own moods, it will also make it more likely. This is also true in your personal lives. Be the bringer of hope, not of sadness and you will be always welcome.

Dear World

20th January

River deep, mountain high, from the depths to the heights. Sometimes in life we flow along the river of life, taking things as they come. At times, the river flows fast and strong, at others slow and gentle. We may not know what is around the bend, but we learn to navigate around or deal with what we find. So, what about the mountain? You ask. Climbing to the heights gives vision and perspective. The effort of it gives satisfaction. This is true both in physical and spiritual terms and like all activities it becomes easier with practice. Many know how to reach the mountains, but struggle on the way down. This is a skill that needs to be mastered, for in life you need to return to the river at times, but at least when you do you may know more of what may lie around the bend.

Dear World

21ˢᵗ January

Gender and sexuality are more fluid than we may think. There exists male and female in all. This expression has usually sided one way or another according to physical gender and cultural expectation. As acceptability and culture changes, the desire and freedom to express different spectrums on the gender scale come more to the fore. We see some problems with this and some gains. Gender confusion can affect development in life and finding a path. Cultural trend can lead to regrettable choices. There are many ways to express our male and female sides and their needs. The way we dress is only one part of this, but exploration is part of discovering this.

Dear World

22/1/20

Love and marriage is an institution of good renown, made and given with good intent. Most enter into it with that same good intent, but others too easily. It saddens you when it fails or falls apart, but there are many reasons for this, not least of which is the other partner. There are also many other influences on the union of two people however much in love they began. We develop at different speeds and different ways. Some paths move apart, that is no judgment on those paths, but it can make the union more strained. Love of course is the key. If you can love beyond the differences, or wait for paths to realign, then all well and good. We feel it is equally acceptable to love in separation if you are strong enough to do so. Move beyond any conflict or blame, especially where children are involved. Love lives beyond separation, both in new love and old love, remember this.

Dear World

23rd January

The end of the road has come in terms of our present existence on this planet. That does not mean death and terror for all. It means consciousness change and therefore world changes. Some will lag behind as always and cling on to the worn-out ways. Much preparation has taken place and many of you have been part of this. Do not be sad for what has gone. What is to come will be better. Do not hold your breath in anticipation, for outer change follows inner change in all conscious beings. What do you need to do you ask? Be still at times and feel. Allow the change. This should not feel jarring to those of you who shine and see the light. Look for the signs and smile with acknowledgement. Nothing lasts forever.

Dear World

24th January

Healing of self seems a difficult thing. Sometimes we feel too close to the problem to be objective about its cause. We do however, know ourselves better than any doctor. Intuitively we may decide that lifestyle or diet choices are paying us back. Maybe we are being protected by creating an illness to get out of something that is not wanted or good for us. This may all be well hidden from our conscious mind of course, but the restriction of illness gives us time to ponder. Sometimes the realisation can speed up the cure or diagnosis. Love and care for yourself as you would another is always the best way.

Dear World

25th January

Surviving and making ends meet can be a worry and constant battle. There are of course degrees of perception of need. In your modern western world, your expectations of comfort and necessities of life are more than of those in a third world country, but nevertheless they are the basis of your participation in your society. It is a root thing. You naturally want to do more than survive. You want to have a bit more to do exploration, give to others and have peace of mind to contemplate spiritual and philosophical matters. When life was all about survival did your ancestors have no spiritual life? In fact, they were very much tuned into the spiritual dimension, because they learned that survival and getting by relied on this connection. One is born of the other. When our livelihood or survival is threatened, tuning to the spiritual dimension for inspiration, insight and hope is natural and has always been so.

Dear World

26th January

There are many stories hidden in the landscape around us, if we only sit a while and listen to their tale. The spirit of the land speaks, as do we, of history and comings and goings that have passed. Of spring and stone, of mound and stream and of buildings old we speak. The walls, the earth and waters remember and spirit to spirit we read their echoes across the years as though time has stood still. Take time at these special places. Be still, ask the question and believe the answers. Allow the dialogue to flow. You may also be given images. If it is given, you come in peace and respect, so be grateful and accept what you receive warmly. Remember, your presence maybe a gift for future travellers. We are all present, past and future revealed.

Dear World

27th January

We think with our heads and feel with our bodies. Our thoughts and feelings are not always aligned. Our head wants to go one way, our body another and our neck feels the pressure. So, what is the answer to this problem? Maybe you should let your head and mind feel and your body think. This awakens your instinctive, primeval and intuitive self. It also helps restore the body-mind balance and reawaken the body's intelligence that knows what it needs at this time.

Dear World

28th January

Anxiety is a condition that many of you suffer from at times. It is a nervous condition of apprehension over the fulfilment of something often out of your control. There is also anxiety about returning to a state of anxiety experienced before. Even when you have moved through previous problems, many doubt faith in yourselves and the spiritual connection to help a situation or feeling pass. We understand that the trigger for anxiety is not always obvious, which can make it feel even worse. So how can we help you? If you feel the anxiety coming on, take a moment, feel it, acknowledge it with love and let it disperse. You may have to repeat this several times, then pause, relax and turn your energy to something that you can have a positive effect upon.

Dear World

29th January

Balance is important between all things in life. Balance between physical, mental, emotional and spiritual activity needs to be considered, although the spiritual permeates all others to some degree. An intellectual person needs to go for long walks to ground those ideas for example. There are times when you need to submerse yourself in a particular state of being, or it may be forced upon you by circumstances. Taking time out, maybe for laughter or a change of scenery or activity can help stop depletion on that plane of action. This helps increase longevity and endurance in your tasks. A good friend or family member may remind you of this need, but it pays to be aware of your own intuition and look for the signs that tell you a break or change is needed. Often when this is not heeded it is forced upon you by illness or injury.

Dear World

30th January

Let us talk about destiny. You will understand this as the fulfilment of your potential in this life on earth. You may also imagine it to be about big actions that outwardly affect a lot of people. Of course, everything we do affects all others at some scale, but in terms of destiny it may be an apparent small thing or a constant thing repeated that is your destiny. For some their destiny is to live a short life, but in that life they may teach others the value of love or acceptance of death. For others, their destiny is large in terms of world events. They may appear good or bad in historical terms, but mainly they are catalysts for change in evolution of humanity, the planet and consciousness. For many of you at this time your destiny may be quiet and unheralded in outward recognition, but nonetheless huge in terms of impact on your mother earth and even beyond. Carry on doing those things that feel right and bright, for in them lies your destiny.

Dear World

31st January

Conspiracy theories abound and they are all based on fears of some kind. The feeling that you are not in control of your own life and that another is manipulating it for their own ends. If you believe it to be true it will be true for you. It is the modern manifestation of age-old superstitions. We are aware of course that not everybody's motivations, whether they be individual, corporate or government, are entirely altruistic, but there are spiritual measures in place that mitigate any extremes of violation occurring. Those trying to push the world in these certain ways could argue that the spiritual forces that curtail them are a controlling force on them. You have free-will it is true, but there are those who guide you in human and spirit form that try and maintain individual and group evolution along the preferred lines. It obviously pays to be aware of malevolent forces, but do not fear them, because they cannot overcome an enlightened soul.

Dear World

1st February

Let us consider that lost and found. Sometimes you lose things for a while and go crazy trying to find them. You were sure they were in a certain place, but they are nowhere to be seen. Where do they go? How do you find them? Feel yourself holding the item in your hands and looking at it. Feel its presence. Now visualise it shining in white light and let the worry of it go from your conscious mind. Let it be found in its own time.

Dear World

2nd February

Home is where the heart is, the saying goes. If you feel your heart open when you enter your home, that is obviously a good thing. It may be more important than location, décor and number of rooms. People need to move for different reasons of course in their lifetime. Unfortunately, in your world homes have become too pricey for many, even those that grew up in an area. This is breaking up many communities and larger family bonds, destabilising wider society. This balance needs to be re-addressed if society is to move forward. We understand your home at this time may be your only security, but is your heart there.

Dear World

3rd February

Planes, trains and automobiles. Transport is changing and needs to quite quickly, but you cannot all keep up. As always, there is a cost individually and also for business and governments. You are transforming to a cleaner world in terms of energy, but this is not just about less pollution and carbon emissions. The energy of our systems of infrastructure relate to our systems of communication. This in turn relates to new and more refined ways of energy exchange and transfer, meaning your thoughts, feelings and exchanging of ideas. This process is quickening exponentially and yes, your world climate crisis is a catalyst for this. The change though is an evolutionary one and needed to happen at this time. Not everything happens at once, but inventions and inspirations are happening as we speak here now. Changes will happen when they become available or affordable, so encourage the change, but do not fret for that which is currently beyond your reach.

Dear World

4th February

Let us talk about occupation. Occupation is used to represent your job and means of employment generally. If you think about it, your occupation is the main way in which you occupy your time. For many that may be for monetary reward, but for others it may be voluntary or inner work that fulfils this role. All areas are of value to society as a whole. It is how they are valued by yourself that is often the question. There is always the feeling that if you were not spending so much of your time doing this one thing you could be doing another. How do you value your occupation? Does it give you satisfaction or a warm glow? Does it spiritually uplift in some way? This is true whatever area you work in. Do not be fooled by appearances. Be honest in your appraisal of self and others in this matter.

Dear World

5th February

Group activities and circles are good for the soul, because they help you to see something in yourself and others that is deeper than the personality you present to the everyday world. When one among you speaks their truth or wisdom, it gives the others permission to do the same. As trust and continuity develops, the otherworldly connections become more apparent and influential. This spiritual law is why it is important to set good intent and earthly grounding at all times. There is nothing supernatural about this process. It is as natural as childbirth or the wind that blows. This is true of the most innocent of groups and the most intensive. As long as it feels true to you it is well to maintain that connection. Group work may by its very nature, throw up challenges at times, but in being mutually supportive through these challenges the group can create a template for our role in wider society. Remember that no man is an island.

Dear World

6th February

The feminine divine often referred to as the goddess or goddesses, is a profound and beautiful reality; the oft denied aspect of spirituality in many formal religions. The wise and earthy know this not to be so of course. Traditionally mankind has called upon the goddess in childbirth, fertility of women and crops and other nurturing roles. At these times it is important to remember that the feminine aspect is not just for women to understand. She governs the receptive side of all of us and is most easily understood in the guise of mother earth, but the earth is in many ways abused. Many of you will already realise that teaching the sacredness of the earth and feminine is essential in restoring equilibrium to the natural and human world. The land and the seas are imbued with spirit, usually viewed as feminine. Imbuing this with the same love and respect you would for your own mother will ensure a more sustainable way forward.

Dear World

7th February

Interaction between the living and the dead, I use those words as most people understand them. Of course, there is no absolute death, just transformation to a different plane. In your societies there are various taboos, depending on culture, about when and who can make contact with those in spirit. It is good for you to remember that you are all free to make this contact if you are willing and able. There are times of course when you will want to concentrate on your earthly relationships and life, but the thoughts and feelings that you have are felt in the spirit world and they are concerned with all your development. This is true in terms of family and friend connections, but also in those who guide you in relation to your own spiritual development and that of the earth and humanity in general. You will all feel and make that connection in different ways, but once you are aware of that helping hand you will know how to read the signs. There are of course those among you who make that connection more readily and you may choose to use their help, but always trust your own intuition and inner guidance in relationship to any messages received. We are here to help, but not to live your life for you.

Dear World

8th February

Let us consider age and new beginnings. Whatever age you are in years, you may at times feel old in your mind or body. One or the other becomes set in its ways, stiff and aches. It pays to keep body and mind as agile and responsive as you can. Obviously as years roll by there is some wear and slowing down, but do not let the negative thoughts, in regard to this, override the physical abilities. Try to have an expectation of renewal and lightness. You are never too old to start something new or change your outlook on life. The key is to let go of what is weighing you down, be that possessions, thoughts or feelings. If you have repeating negative thoughts in regard to your abilities, ask yourself; 'Do I still own these thoughts?' 'Do they still serve who I now am?' Let the answers to these questions guide how you move forward.

Dear World

9th February

Today we talk about the weather. It may be increasingly wild and extreme at these times. The weather is elemental. There are god forces that have dominion over it, but they are in turn governed by, or serve, mother earth. The elements are also tied to the moods of the planet and all upon it. They serve to create balance in nature, but also in regard to the elements in life on earth, our emotions, passions and so on. The more that is out of balance, the more extreme the weather events need to be, to highlight it or bring it back into balance. These forces are not beyond being affected by enlightened human or spiritual intent, but ultimately they are subject to their main function of keeping nature and earth in balance. However, like us they are subject to the higher power that encourages spiritual evolution on earth. Those elemental forces will therefore remind humanity when it wanders from its path, as historic myths and stories are keen to remind us.

Dear World

10th February

Sometimes when we awaken, or re-awaken to our spiritual responsibility, it can feel a burden, a weight on our shoulders and minds. Depending on your awareness, it can be quite clear what you need to do at a spiritual level in terms of helping the required change on the earth plane. You also have to make a living and live your day-to-day life and deal with its problems and celebrate its joys. 'Surely I can't do all of this' you say. We say you can, but we would wouldn't we. You are never alone in this work, although at times you may feel that you are. Even at these times there is a time to play and a time to pray. There are times to be alone and times to be with others. When you feel the weight of responsibility and the isolation that can bring taking hold, perform this exercise. Take time to connect inwardly to all those in your world who feel the same and then send them the love, support and healing that you need yourself. The circle of light will be strengthened by this loving act.

Dear World

11th February

How do we learn? How do children learn? In schools and classrooms, yes of course that is true, but also in play and questioning. Also, in observing, especially those close to them. A child's appetite for knowledge is as voracious as their appetite for food at times. Why? They ask. As adults we answer the best we can and in doing so realise how much we accept ourselves without questioning. Maybe like the child we eventually got tired of asking why, because we stopped getting answers. Never stop giving the best answers to those who ask something of you and never stop questioning why. In questioning why something has always been so, can come the breakthrough that removes stagnation and opens up minds. If your questions are satisfied it consolidates tradition and bonds.

Dear World

12th February

Let us talk about the flow of money in the world. It can be blocked by fear, greed or feelings of unworthiness. Also, old karmic ties to lives or vows of poverty can lead to guilt in accumulating any kind of wealth in this life. Previous lives of poverty happened in order to teach you the value of non-material assets like love, but also to appreciate money and use it wisely when received. Sometimes the flow of money may be temporarily restricted due to illness or the restrictive process needed to learn greater lessons or assimilate them. We know this can be frustrating and seem counter intuitive, because your mind becomes over occupied with concerns over money. Experience and maturity in life and soul life helps you to discern when this is so.

So, what can increase the flow of money? Specific needs, especially if for greater benefit, can usually enhance the flow, as can confidence and self-belief in the worthiness to receive. We of course encourage personal spiritual service and growth, but we recognise the need to nurture and satisfy the personality enough that good work is continued with renewed vigour and energy. Money is a token for energy given and received, although in some cases there may be some distance from the energetic exchange to the monetary one. This is another way in which the current earth has become unbalanced. As with all things, give with love and receive with love.

Dear World

13th February

We all have animal guides or helpers. They are guardians of our souls. They are especially active when we are in unconscious or partially conscious states, as when under the influence of anaesthetics, drugs or alcohol. This is one reason why people sometimes behave in a primal way under these conditions. The animal spirit is trying to protect the soul from its vulnerability in these situations. You can most readily contact your spirit animal by inner journeying, usually to what is known as the underworld or lower world, consciously going below in a meditative state. As well as their personal relationships with our individual soul, we also have animal familiars connected to our family and ancestral lines. The observant among you may notice this in the characteristics of certain family groups. In tribal communities this fact is outwardly acknowledged in tribal totems. In your modern world the idea of an animal spirit may seem outdated, but it is still very much needed. As protector of the soul, it recognises when you are shrivelling up due to monotonous or unrewarding work, unnatural surroundings, or destructive habits. Your animal guide will help you gather back your disparate soul and restore the energy you need to create a life more in tune with the needs of your soul in this lifetime.

Dear World

14th February

What is the point of a virus or cold? Our immune system needs to be worked in order to be ready to function when needed in extreme illness or infection. You are constantly being exposed to viruses and bacteria and these organisms live within you, as you yourself live within the wider organism of your earthly surroundings. A virus will adapt rapidly in order to survive and multiply and your immune system will adapt to survive its attack. It is interesting to note that a virus does not want its host to die. The virus will survive better and spread more if the host is well enough to encounter other people and to live on. A young child will show the symptoms of many colds and viruses. We should not be worried by this, because it shows that its immune system is developing well. This adaption of the immune system teaches our whole organism to adapt to its changing environment more readily. So, although a virus can be an annoyance, be grateful to some extent, because it is priming you to be ready to adapt to change and other threats to health and well-being.

Dear World

15th February

Ancestral influence is strong at these times, in the darker months of the year. That has always been so. In the origins of human religion they called out to those who had passed in death, to their chiefs, leaders and mothers to help and guide them. They had deep connection to the land where they lived and in death could remain close, if that was their intention. It evolved that those who were adept at communicating with them became the seers and priests. The ancestors taught them of spiritual realms and tried to hold influence there in order to help their descendants on earth. In early times the connection was difficult and an exchange or gift of sacrifice was employed to raise the energy. It is well known that in all societies this practice became abused in later years, but it was a necessary stage of progress. This is no longer needed as the connections are many and the medium of communication is more electrical in nature, as befits the changes on the earth plane. Ancestors are still the initial contact with spirit, because we can usually trust that they have our best interests at heart. They use their connection with you, the living, to bring continuity and security, but also to open a door to spiritual influence from higher realms. Remember them well.

Dear World

16th February

The unknowing of things has occurred from time to time in history from the earliest of times. This is the unknowing of past wisdom for the sake of new knowledge. You could say 'throwing the baby out with the bath water'. It is in the nature of much of humanity to do this. A new theory or invention answers many questions, so it is gradually adopted and the old wisdom is regarded as primitive or old fashioned, so it falls out of use. This is a mistake, because in all ages of life on earth there is wisdom to behold. Even that which to modern eyes seems superstitious, contains truths about archetypal energies and mythic beings, which can explain as much about present day happenings as can modern science or technology. At this time, as technology evolves exponentially, there is an equal interest in looking to the wisdom of the past. It is true that not everything is still relevant, but if we look at old wisdom and truths through the prism of our current existence, we can soon realise what shines through. You, the wisdom-keepers who know these truths may be called upon to disseminate and share your knowledge to those who seek it honestly. Be discerning, but be open, for it is much needed.

Dear World

17th February

Shadows of the past wash over you. By this we mean the emotional trauma of past hurts that still affect your life now. These shadows can range from fear to apprehension, apathy or self-loathing. We all learn through life experience, but in the human condition the emotional memory of an event or encounter can be more powerful than the event itself. So, when you encounter a similar situation, or feel that you may do so, you create blocks to moving forward. None of us likes being hurt, or failing in an endeavour, so we protect ourselves. If we have demons, we need to face them. Is there behaviour we need to change? Do we need to be better prepared? Doing the same thing in the same way usually gets the same results. If you felt that you failed the first time, then next time do it differently, do it better or do something else. This may seem a little harsh, but it is about being honest with yourself. In this way you throw light on the shadows that follow you.

Dear World

18th February

Teaching is an art and a gift to give. Whether you are a professional teacher, or one who passes on lessons of life, the same parameters apply. The first lesson is to teach the desire to learn and be curious, for this can last a lifetime. The next lesson is how to understand, for in all things this is important. Aligned with this is practice and experience, for these assimilate knowledge into our understanding. Learning to be kind, tolerant and understanding the different ways in which we all learn, is an art that is desirable to master. You will be well thanked for this. To teach many, in different ways at the same time, takes experience, understanding, empathy and patience. It is a spiritual lesson as well as a life lesson, for are we all not unique, but also of the same light of being.

Dear World

19th February

Courage takes many forms. For some it takes great courage just to go out of the door and leave the house. For others they need courage to stand up for what they believe in. The courage to fight through an illness, overcome job loss, bereavement or abuse is a wondrous thing. It is difficult for the outsider to see the courage needed in another, either for simple or great tasks. Courage is in the heart of the beholder. In other words, we are all climbing mountains at times, even if we have scaled the summit before. The setbacks of life and a humbleness of soul may cause you to question; who am I to do or say this? If you set your eyes upon a greater truth and look beyond your own fears, then you become part of a movement of irresistible force and momentum that lifts you up and carries you in its wake.

Dear World

20th February

What are you missing? There is something you cannot quite understand in the nature of the changes around you. The scientists give you facts and figures and possible, even probable scenarios. We give you clues to spiritual impulses behind current world changes, but still you feel there is some other factor at play. There is of course, fate. Fate is the outcomes set in motion by previous events, actions and impulses, but seemingly out of your control. Discerning what is fate and what we do have the power to change, is not always easy. You do not want to waste your energy on futile actions. Trial and error will eventually help you to decide if fate is at play, but also intuition will help you accept what is fate and be gracious in acceptance. You can then direct your energy to where you can make a difference. Do not be told that acceptance is giving up or apathy; for we know how much you will fight when positive change is a potential outcome. Who or what ultimately decides your fate is to be pondered and meditated on for another day.

Dear World

21st February

Illumination is the light of spirit that connects with the light of the heart. When something shines with this light, it awakens to your consciousness and triggers a recognition in your heart. As light is consciousness, illumination is the raising of that light to a level of truth that is recognised by the soul. When there is some shadow or block in your life, or the life of those around you, shine the light of consciousness upon it. Things will become clearer and if you are blessed, we in spirit may illuminate the matter, if it is desirable and appropriate. You may associate illumination with gods and angels, but it is nearer to your reach than you might imagine. Where consciousness of your soul meets consciousness of light, illumination is at hand.

Dear World

22nd February

Group work is important in these becoming times. Humanity's evolution requires awareness of the exponential power of the group and community to make change. The current crisis facing all on earth is at one level the fault of mankind, but on another it is a reflection of the workings of spirit. The anxieties and desire to have support and make positive change creates the impulse for group development. Individual work is of course still important, but the group work can make the magic happen. This gradual realisation of that powerful dynamic will change the conscious way we look at any individual, group or world problem. You do have to find the best groups to fit your own dynamics of course, but do not fear taking steps. Just be drawn to where you feel most at home.

Dear World

23rd February

The spirit of trees is strong. They have a spirit which lives in all three of the shamanic worlds; below in the underworld, above in the upper world and in the middle world around us. Their roots, branches and trunk allow them to do this. They connect to and message each other mainly through their roots, but also through the air that touches their leaves. They are aware of all life of the forest and of you. Their longevity and deep roots feeds into a wisdom beyond that of humans. You can though, with practice and respect, build up a relationship and connection with a tree. Their aura is wide, so feel it as you approach. Walk sunwise and wait for them to welcome you in. Their large spirit will help you to develop and trust your own spiritual being and in time the tree will be a good ally in your care and protection of the earth. In return, your love for the trees means that you will do what you can towards their protection. Many of you have lived the lives of trees, so know what strengths and gifts they bring.

Dear World

24th February

Sound healing is an ancient art. Its practitioners were trained in the art and skill of listening to an individual's vibration and to feel where it was out of balance. This is like tuning a piano. They then used voice, drum, or other instrument to reset the balance. This is a practice that is coming back into favour. We are pleased with this. There are different harmonics in the universe. The universal spirit uses them to try and attune individuals to a better vibration for their path. When you do sound healing work on yourself or others, you can tune into these harmonic resonances to aid and enhance your work. When several come together in this work it becomes easier and more powerful to achieve this connection. Sound can penetrate body, mind, soul and spirit to restore, rejuvenate and establish new positive connections between each other and other worlds of existence.

Dear World

25th February

In life there are always disappointments. What you believe is going to happen does not materialise. What is it that causes materialisation anyway? Is it you? Is it other people? If you can imagine something happening, then it is more likely to happen if not certain to. If you cannot even imagine it, then it is unlikely to occur. Creation needs input from the imaginary and visionary realms. Things are also affected by your thoughts, emotions and beliefs and those of others. If someone feels unworthy or undeserving, they may block a pleasurable experience from happening. There are also spiritual parameters around us all. They may at times feel imposed, but ultimately they are always with agreement from your own self. Past conditioning and habits may make any of you misinterpret these parameters. Life is for living, just ensure you keep up with your spiritual promises along the way.

Dear World

26th February

Where does knowledge come from? Every thought ever had exists somewhere in the ether ready to be enfolded by your mind and transmuted by your brain into expression. Obviously if that same thought is or was had by many, then it has more power and more likely to be picked up. This is also true if it comes from a particular powerful source, whether it be incarnate human or spirit. It is much like your internet of today. There are enormous amounts of knowledge available, but no guarantee of truth, morality or accuracy. Wherever you receive your thoughts from, they need first to be tested against the light of your own truth and values. Also, if appropriate, they should be wielded against rational and scientific considerations. If that knowledge still stands up to practice and experience, even if only to you, then it is true knowledge and will in time be passed on, for that is how knowledge is disseminated. Wisdom is knowing where, when and if to apply knowledge and that is a matter for another time.

Dear World

27th February

Prophecy as we have said before is a fluid thing. It depends on the trajectory of the soul through this life, but also in relation to other past lifetimes. The past, or its perception, can be changed. This affects the present, which in turn affects future possibilities. This holds true for individuals, but also for nations, the planet and life as a whole. There is a saying; 'Nothing is written in stone.' Of course, sometimes it is literally, but stone can erode, crack, be buried and later re-exposed. This is all a metaphor for the past, which is constantly informing the present and therefore future creation. Do not be tied down by other people's doomsday scenarios or tales of woe. The future may be brighter than you think.

Dear World

28th February

Immunity around the world varies towards different pathogens. Immunity comes through exposure and response of the immune system to produce anti-bodies to that pathogen. Eventually vaccines can help in the process, but the adaption of humanity individually and as a whole, builds up resistance. A global virus is a rare thing, but it does make humanity realise how much they are connected, for good or bad. It also highlights the situations and concentrations of people that encourage the rapid spread of infection. Individual immunity depends upon a number of factors. Diet is paramount, as in a healthy diet especially of fresh fruit and vegetables, preferably close to source and uncontaminated by pesticides. Also age and general health are important. Breast feeding and exposure to common ailments when young, help to develop this immunity. Sometimes the body will allow a mild virus or bacterial infection in for a while if adaption to it helps the body build resistance to more serious infections. The vulnerable need to be protected where possible. Nature is always trying to find homeostasis and balance. Humanity is part of that equation. Life is precious, but so is life of the planet, your home.

Dear World

29th February

There are mysteries hidden beneath the streets and along the waterways of this land, also along the hedgerows, lanes and woods of the country. It is heard in the tales of the old ones and the imagination of the young ones. Openings to a reality seen by the few, oblivious to the masses. There is a richness of history, legend and layers of belonging that connect people to places and give root to abstract thoughts. Like attracts like. The artists and artisans return to the workshops of forgotten craftsmen. Old stores and warehouses give rise to fresh cooked cuisine from exotic shores. The wheel keeps turning. Nothing is forgotten for ever; it just changes its hue and sometimes rests a while. Life is a rich tapestry woven from generations past, present and yet to come.

Dear World

1st March

Truth, honesty and transparency in spiritual teachings are important. There are a myriad of sources available on spiritual matters and it is difficult for the individual to discern what is best for them. In some ways this is why organised religions developed, leading to guidelines of accepted teachings, others being rejected as heresy. Although not ideal, this development did help the general spread of spiritual awareness and moral values. In the present times humanity is looking for a more individual expression of spiritual truth, although they may still wish to celebrate with others on similar paths or having common aims.

We are encouraging those of you who are honest seekers, to express your spiritual truth as perceived through your own connection to spirit. It is important that you explain that it is the truth as given to you and expressed in the way acceptable to you. If it is called for, you are free to explain what is given to the best of your ability. It is up to others how much they accept in part or in total, reject or use as a basis for discussion. There are absolute truths of course, but it is the explanation of their manifestation that causes some problems. The main goal in showing your truth is to encourage others to seek and express theirs. We encourage you to express and share this truth with love and respect for all. Peace be with you.

Dear World

2nd March
The mother looks after her own. The mother earth goddess cares for her spirit children. Being spiritual in this life on earth counts for nothing if you are not trying to live a life that acknowledges the sacredness of earth and all on it. Those who live in care of her, despite the limitations that modern life brings, are blessed. At this time many of you are sad. Do not be, we wrap you in our arms and pray with you for the best to come. She holds you to her breast. Hold onto what you believe and value the fellowship in others. It is still ok to rest in the blessing of the goddess. We are watching over her as she watches over you.

Dear World

3rd March

Soul growth is not inevitable, but it is desirable and always encouraged from above. Sometimes a soul becomes tired of that pushing onwards with spiritual ideals in mind. We understand this and as in all things, it is acceptable to have a break and a breather now and then. Your soul is constantly learning, whatever you do. Bringing those lessons into consciousness may take a little longer. You may look at some and think they have little development of soul or are slipping backwards. This may not be so. Karma is learning through experience and a soul may need to see life from the shadow side for its ultimate growth. We are all on different stages of the wheel and it pays to be humble and understanding of all, whatever role they are playing.

Dear World

4th March

Let us talk about sex. Controversial I know. Why do you desire sexual interaction? There is a lowering then raising of energy when you just think about it. Of course, in some spiritual teachings sex is painted as evil, or at least undesirable, save in the basic need to procreate. It is true the abuse of sex and disregarding its consequences are worrying and to be avoided. Sexual union is a divine act, an energetic exchange and a sharing of intimacy. In the ecstatic act of orgasm, energy rises from the root up through the chakras and opening the crown chakra. If undertaken consciously, with mutual respect for each other, then it can be very powerful as a spiritual and magical act. Regardless of the genders participating, it is in essence the union of the earth goddess and sky father, but also potentially our own yin and yang, the merging of our masculine and feminine sides. Of course, sex provides other earthly and emotional needs, but in the sacred union its gifts and blessings can spread beyond those involved.

Dear World

5th March

Changes in climate, life and the world around you are happening now. You are living in a far different world from even only a year ago in many ways. Internal and external changes feel like the new norm. Depending on your mood and viewpoint you either; hold onto the old, embrace the new or remain frozen in a state of fear and apathy. It is not for you to know all the reasons why. As man changes through the ages of life, so the earth changes through cycles of its own incarnations. In this epoch the souls of humans are linked to the earth mother soul. It is then inevitable that you will feel and ride these thresholds of transformation with her. While humanity may appear to be the cause of change, you are only in the sense that viruses change your own individual dynamic. There is always another force initiating the process. It is your nature to question, but sometimes it is best to understand what you can and leave the rest to chance, fate and love of god and goodness.

Dear World

6th March

Remembering our gifts and blessings is an act of praise and thanksgiving in itself. Sometimes in your hectic lives you are always looking for the next thing to do or place to go. This is all well and good and we admire your enthusiasm for life, but taking time to count your blessings and be grateful is good practice. Also, in remembering your gifts you are acknowledging not only what you receive from the world, but also your own gifts that you share with others. Remembering itself is a lesson in re-centring. Sometimes in remembering your current gifts you may get a feeling of what gifts are dormant in your soul from previous lives, waiting to be revealed. They only need the stimulus of an outer need, combined with an inner awakening. Pay heed to an expression that appears new but feels familiar. Life is forever re-inventing itself.

Dear World

7th March

Many people are spiritually seeking at this time. They take their knowledge and wisdom from many sources. This is a good thing, but at some point most ask if it is desirable to follow a certain path. A spiritual path is a pathway of certain teachings and sometimes initiations that slowly open up the follower to wisdom and different aspects of consciousness and spirit. It should also help you to make your own relationship with spiritual guidance. It has the benefit of the blessings of many who have trodden these steps before and can open you up to a wisdom stream that may be ancient in origin.

There are times on a path when you are very focused on that path, but at others you feel free to explore other paths for their teachings and practices which are in harmony with your own. There is wisdom in all paths, including the path of the wandering spiritual explorer. Sometimes though, following a specific path can enable community and the easier expression of spiritual knowledge in appropriate action, healing or teaching.

Dear world

8th March

The urge to travel can sometimes be strong. You may feel drawn to a certain place, particular people or maybe a gathering or event. We know you caring ones are trying to reduce your impact on planet earth and we applaud you for that. If you are being frugal and careful in avoiding pollution when you can, then do not be guilty for travelling when it lifts the spirits, or engages you with like-minded souls. A certain amount of travel is allowed for as we transition to a cleaner energy source. Everything happens in stages. Use what is available, just use it wisely. Flying is a luxury in terms of its impact. There are many reckless ones in this respect and wasteful processes. It is for them to change, not you. A rare flight may be part of your plan and in so being, not the end of the world. We know you feel the need to walk the walk as well as talk the talk, but in showing others that extremes are not what is required at this time, you show others that change is possible for them. When many change their habits a little, great change is possible.

Dear World

9th March

Collective fear and panic is a contagious thing. Many in your society like to be told what to do, but are then paranoid about being controlled. Fear is a reaction to potential harm that appears to be out of your control. In some ways, society is addicted to fear. They watch films, television programmes and games that engender fear or horror. In some ways this may be a reaction to the sterilization and banality of modern life. You can manage your own fear and apprehension to some degree.

Look at what you do have control over. For example; where you go, who you encounter and what you do. Also look after your diet and exercise. Be discerning over what information you take in, beware of sensationalism. That which you have little or no control over, deal with when you need to. Have a plan in hand if required, then be calm and save your energy for when it is needed. Take sensible precautions and take care of those others that need care and advice. Have faith in yourself and others to do the right thing.

Dear World

10th March

The healer among you is a wise one, sometimes hidden from view. The veils of perception, when traversed, can take their toll. There are times of withdrawal to gain knowledge and strength, especially at times of change. The healer knows himself, but doubts himself at times, because not all can be healed, least of all that which pains him or herself. The search for the cure is what teaches them and leads them on. Nothing is as simple as it seems. Deeper healing takes time and commitment. Those that undertake its work are watched over. The healers and teachers of spirit help and also learn from those on earth. All evolves together. As we have said before, the seen and unseen are mutually dependent, if spiritually independent. Bless the healers, for there is much healing to be done.

Dear World

11th March

Life, death and what lies beyond have been mused upon for centuries. The meaning of life is the material of philosophers, priests and magicians. You make the error of assuming that there is only one aim and meaning for your life on earth. There is a multiplicity and not all are for your individual benefit. Yes, life helps develop the qualities of a soul, through experience and relationship with others. Life may also mean putting aside that personal development for a while in order to further the path of humanity's growth and the unfolding of the earth experiment. This sounds like science fiction to you maybe, but it is true that certain parameters have been encouraged on earth to further the seed of growth of a universal idea. This means ultimately, consciousness made incarnate and how that functions when engaged with other conscious life at complex and different levels of awareness and need.

You must not think of yourselves as guinea pigs in this plan, but volunteers involved with its outcome. Awareness at this level of consciousness is as real as your awareness of your physical life and all its pleasures and problems. Integration of what some call super consciousness and everyday consciousness are in some ways the challenge of the present times.

Dear World

12th March

How do you live all of you? How do you make a living? How do you earn your crust? An occupation is your means of spending time productively, you hope with some financial reward or at least reward in kind. In the current world there is a need for money to pay for everything from housing to food, transport and a myriad of other things like insurance and household bills. Some of you like to imagine a world where this constant reliance on earning and spending was no longer necessary. This world already exists in one sphere of reality, but you on earth may not be ready for its lack of belonging or ownership. The ownership of place and objects gives spirit in human form a rootedness and fixation in the material world. This is part of living on earth, but it is for humanity to decide the level of ownership and possession that gives a living experience without compensating spiritual freedom. It is not always an easy balance to find individually and even less so collectively. It is important not to be too angry or frustrated over the present situation, but accept it for how it is at this time. Change is always afoot.

Dear World

13th March

Superstition is the stuff of myths and legends or unfortunate historical events. 'Friday the 13th, unlucky for some.' You may know it is associated with the Knights Templar and their demise under the edict of the King of France. 'Beware the ides of March' was the warning prophecy given to Caesar and it was the middle of March when he was murdered. So, is there any truth in superstitious beliefs? It would seem for them to persist for so long there may be so. Of course, if the belief that a certain date or action is unlucky finds its way into the collective consciousness, then when bad things happen as a result of that action or on that date, they will be remembered. This is so even if many good or normal things happen also on those dates or following those actions.

Superstition often arises because the masses realise that there are underlying forces or intelligence shifting the patterns of life. If they do not have the knowledge or understanding to assign the causal factors, they will create beliefs about which scapegoats or figures of authority are controlling matters. If enough start to believe this it seems to be truth to many. The personal seekers of wisdom and true spiritual connection endeavour to find meaning for unusual events and happenings that satisfy their own truth. This courage of independent thought and belief usually holds them in good stead in the long run.

Dear World

14th March

So, what is the message of the virus? Are you not all the same when faced with this illness? You all bleed and you all die at some point. When there is nowhere to hide, money or walls make no difference to your vulnerability in the long run. You are being shown that the world is one. World problems are not only for you alone, but for all to work together on. A virus knows how to change, adapt and pass on. Is that not its message to us? To be prepared to change for the whole, for in the whole earth lies our destiny. Do not be sad for what is passing. Hold hands in unity and love. As you were born out of the smallest of organisms, so shall you be reborn. Nothing lasts for ever. Even the best laid plans can falter. The sooner we embrace the wholeness, the sooner life returns. There is no death anyway, only continuity of evolved existence.

Dear World

15th March

Those inside the bubble are already feeling the new. You are enveloped in the new energy and the light shines upon you. Overcome the fear and realise that sometimes that which you fear the most, brings the best healing. The light shines down upon you children of spirit. Wise ones, shining ones, the Earth arises anew. Place one foot in front of another and walk onward. Yours is the birth-right of champions of soul. Do not be sad anymore. Land of joyous virtue is before you.

Dear World

16th March

How do we get through a crisis? Worlds move and shift. As we move from one way to another way of being there is resistance. This is like two tectonic plates rubbing against each other, causing earthquakes and volcanoes to erupt. It is temporary, but difficult to live through. Hold the new that is becoming in your heart and then deal with what is in front of you. Be kind and be helpful, for there are those in much need of reassurance and loving care. Nature's way is to awaken all to the reality as well as the beauty of existence.

Dear World

17th March

There is always some cause to fight for, but at times like these when you are weary with the strain, you need to surrender into the arms of the goddess. Trust in her care for a while, it is not all up to you. Breathe deeply. Feel your roots sink deep into the earth. Smile a while, feel the steady beat of your heart. You are alive. Nothing is real in the permanent sense. So, some things that feel important now will not feel that way for ever. The temple of the ancient suns is before you; enter at your peril, but without fear. For although there is no certainty beyond its gates, you would not be given the keys if you were not worthy. Blessed are the servants of god and the three-fold goddess.

Dear World

18th March

New beginnings keep being mentioned by us we know, but how does that materialise in individual lives? You are all on a path of loving kindness through a forest of possibilities. There is no right or wrong, only decisions of preference and choice at each crossroads or point of intersection. There is no turning back now, we have come this far. The worst is behind you, despite what some might say. Expect the best outcome and it will be yours alone. Sadly, we do not always know what is best for you, that is why you all have freedom of choice within the realms of destiny given to you.

Dear World

19th March

Look beyond the storm. At these times many are in the middle of the storm running for shelter afraid of the rain, but the rain is cleansing. After a storm, the air is clearer, the grass smells fresh and birds sing. Yes, while the wind blows you need to be strong, take in your sail and take shelter in port, but plans and opportunities are not in vain now. Just take one step at a time.

Dear World

20th March

So as spring begins there is a quickening in the life force. As blossom appears in hedgerows and birds begin to nest, your own energy begins to rise. There is still much to look forward to. As the days grow longer and brighter, optimism begins to conquer fear. Do not be imprisoned by rules. Be sensible and cautious in regard to the welfare of self and others, but do not succumb to the fear of others. Be the light at the end of the tunnel, the candle in the darkness and the rising sun of the morning. If not you, then who? Use the growing energy of earth and sun to strengthen your vitality and encourage that in others.

Dear World

21st March

So as the wheel turns and the year gathers pace there is much to be done, but you are told to hide away. Much still can be done and of course there is much need in the world. Sadness in your eyes needs a home, a safe space of expression. Hearts are heavy after a difficult winter and a restricted spring to look forward to. A narrowing of the path forces focus of mind and spirit. A journey is needed before too long. Let us broaden the horizons to obtain clarity. For clarity is desirable amidst the fog of misinformation and fortune hunters. Be still in the field of peace and perceive the life unfolding.

Dear World

22nd March

It is true that even we in spirit are listening to those above us and we also watch your world and listen to the thoughts of the bright ones on earth. At this critical time, we see the earth in changing swirls of colours. As the virus reaches a critical mass in terms of people infected there is a shift in colour as the required shift in consciousness is made. At this time, the need for the virus in that region is diminished, so it gradually fades. This is not the end of the shift, but an awakening for many and a confirmation for those already aware. Some will not make it. We acknowledge their sacrifice for the greater good. They are the way-showers and will be well cared for. The world has many corners to reach, but it may be that the expansion of the whole and return to truth avoids the need for global reach of this catalyst. Remember also the non-human life, for they are witnesses and partakers in change, yet less troubled by fear.

Dear World

23rd March

Take courage and take heed. We know these times are difficult in so many ways. There is much we see around you and yet who knows which way to turn. You have energy to burn, yet where do you direct it? Let us help you. The times they are a changing, a song you are familiar with. The rule of law is strong and rigid at these times. Fear makes the masses crave instruction. Will surrender to these rules bring the desired result? It is yet to be known, but beware of the price of surrender to authoritarian rule. It has happened before when crisis looms and expediency allows scant reflection. It is well to be wary even though you may be weary of the fight. Remember that for this virus to go away, the bigger change to openness and co-operation must become the normal and accepted means of being.

Dear World

24th March

So, life moves on. What a difference a day makes. Worlds change and countries change. Life is slowing down for most once the nerves have settled. Gone are the days of sales targets and competition for necessities. That which you need for life should not be subject to profit mark ups and share dividends. Do you think this is what the mother goddess wants for her children? The provision of shelter, heating, water and wholesome food need not cost the earth or destroy it. Those who have the means should endeavour to find or grow their own and those who cannot, should be provided for, or allowed to pay in kind or reasonable money. The times are gone for petty squabbles over that which amounts to insignificant differences. Walk on through the storm; it will not last for ever. Be kind to each other, even the angry ones. Keep on moving on.

Dear World

25th March

The next stages are critical in terms of the future outcomes. It is important that governments do not over respond, because this is as dangerous as an immune system over-reacting. The calm and measured response is the right one. Leaders and governments need to hold their nerve as cases and unfortunately deaths peak. Do nothing to increase fear at this stage, then things will begin to turn around. It is important for every one of you to welcome the new, but it requires a certain amount of letting go.

Dear World

26th March

A little light relief maybe what is needed at this time. We know some are suffering, but it does not help for all to suffer. You need to lighten the load at times, refresh, laugh a little and enjoy the life that you can. It does no one good to live too intensely for too long. Remember we are all trying to bring all things back into balance, which means each one of you as well as the planet. Feel your body's needs as well as your mind's needs. The yearnings of spirit for peace, fulfilment and end of suffering are universal, but not achieved overnight. Be kind to yourselves along the path. Breathe deeply and trust in the process.

Dear World

27th March

Softly, softly now, that is the way to go. No need for the constant chatter of no consequence. We could be in this for the long haul, so maybe it is time to pace ourselves. Be mellow and smooth in motion. The dog and cat know when to rest. Learn from them. Allow the light to enter in. There is a time to be fire and a time to be water. When you still the waters of your soul you can bathe in its healing depths. Tomorrow is another day. It will come in its own time. Peace be with you and become you.

Dear World

28th March

So here we are watching and waiting for signs of hope and movement amongst the little actions of individuals playing their part. All are discovering their role in the melodrama; the silent wounded, the action hero or super villain to be vilified. Or maybe you alternate between them all. You ask yourself, am I victim, perpetrator or rescuer? Which shoes fit your questioning soul? The pangs of guilt or confusion need a home, so there you all stay, allowing process to have its run. Be it wrath of god and nature or man's ineptitude, it matters not in the long run. The challenge is for the taking. The gift is for opening. Know yourself and others, whether alone or together. Know the earth and all its life forms are as one in constant motion, moving towards a future yet undreamed. Play your part for today and play it well, for we are all each other's saviour.

Dear World

29th March

Behave in a way which you would like others to follow. Don't be saddened by disaster to the point of immobility, but allow the heart to rule your actions. Heart means courage as well as love, action and deed inspired by greater love. There is a time to hide away and lick our wounds, a time to wallow in the mire, but when recharged return again to re-ignite the fire. These times are strange and murky from above, let alone from your perspective. When you do have some clarity, it needs to be shared, despite the risk of misunderstanding. It would seem the time for reticence is behind us in this respect. If there was ever a time for seers and visionaries is it not now? Look through the window of your soul and let it be known what you see. The days are coming soon when this will all be over and you will look back in anger at opportunities missed if not taken now.

Dear World

30th March

So here we are again, three months have gone, a quarter of the year and so many changes. How many more to come? I hear you asking. Most things have been set in motion. The initial inertia was the most difficult thing to get past. Humanity and human beings are amazingly adaptable given the chance. When you let go of your fears, you have the courage to go where angels fear to tread. It is not for us to judge you or criticize, but only to guide and help as you individually help others. There is time now for new beginnings. Nothing is yet set in stone. You are all co-creators of this world to be. Take a brush in hand and paint a picture in your imagination of what could be, in mutual care for the whole planet. We are one world, one life, one love.

Dear World

31st March

So, this is the end of the month, a long month indeed and where to now. April is the month of spring; new-born lambs, warming days and plans for summer. In this pandemic world it seems a little different, though spring will be sprung. Trees, birds, flowers, butterflies and lambs do not need the permission or attendance of mankind to do their thing. It is not without sadness that some are able to witness this blooming time and other are not, but even without this crisis there are many who were oblivious to this awakening. As there are those blind to the awakening spring, there are many unseeing and unfeeling of this new dawn of earth life. This shift is all too apparent to the observers of nature, because they see it in the nature of humanity and themselves. Celebrate the kindness and togetherness of spirit when you see it. Acknowledgement brings awareness and opening to awareness is raising a change in consciousness. The more who understand and feel this, then the sooner the darkness will pass. Seeing is believing,

---

Dear World

1st April

Here on the other side of the equation things are starting to look a little different. The thought forms are shifting from grey to lighter shades. The mists are still swirling, but the polarity lock is broken open. The immediate time is unstable. New paradigms are forming. Be still a while people and focus on the good in each of you. Be the future you want to see. All beings must take their part.

Dear World

2nd April

There is so much beauty in your world, from the kindness of strangers to birds singing and the abundance of spring flowers. To sit by a flowing brook or spring, or to walk beside a tranquil river are but dreams for some at this time, but to many they were irrelevant or invisible when they were able to travel. Deep in our hearts we know we come from earth and sky and our moods are ruled by the flow of water. This is a simple truth yet denied by so many. If you were born of these life forces and imbued with spirit, is it not the birth-right and destiny of all to preserve and protect them. Those who know this need little reminder, but maybe the blinkered ones will emerge from their cells to wonder anew at life's beauty. That is our hope for you all.

Dear World

3rd April

This is the world. See it, hear it, feel it around you. How real is it? How 'real' are you? There is much to be said for independent living and a solitary life, but humans, like most sentient beings need others to reflect their being. Too much self-reflection can make you crazy, if only temporarily. How are you feeling? Rules are sometimes meant to be broken, controversial I know, but if you cause no risk and no harm it might be ok. At the end of the day people are social creatures and false imprisonment has limited benefits as we see it. Yes, it is good to slow down at times and let your soul catch up with your body, but to go against the turn of the seasons is unnatural.

Dear World

4th April

Dear world we see you now enclosed and surrounded by a shadow. Not as dark and thick as you might think. As you shed your winter duvet or put away your winter coat, so shall you discard this shadow upon your earth. We are surrounding you with so much love, which you may feel in your hearts. We are nearer the threshold of change than you can imagine. The naysayers will be silenced. Lift up your eyes and look up to the skies. As the sun shines, your own sun will shine from within. Do not be afraid of tomorrow or next week, but celebrate today. This is the essence of living in the now, the new and present future to be. My children we are sad for your losses, but we always see beyond your horizon. A new day is dawning. The truth will not be silenced. The wronged will be righted. The army of light marches onwards. There is nothing to be feared that cannot be seen and named. Never be downhearted while the flag of golden truth is held high.

Dear World

5th April

There are indoor people and outdoor people. Usually the indoor people end up telling the outdoor people what to do, but they do not understand their mission and purpose on earth. Those who love the great outdoors intercede between earth and sky, between the earth realms and the place of the gods. Even those that are not conscious of this play a part. You do not defeat an attack by hiding away in fear. What happened in the past? you ask. In those mass pandemics of past centuries there were less medical skills, but many still survived. Their strength lay in their ability to see the bigger picture. They realised that every pandemic has something to teach us and when that is realised healing begins. Leaders have to make decisions and choices, but all things must be balanced. Yes, the abusers of freedom must be punished, but there is much good work that will be lost if all are punished for the sake of a few. Hold onto what is true. Ask how best I can help in this situation. Do not allow yourselves to be brought down by those who do not see the whole truth. We wish you well at this time.

Dear World

6th April

Resilience is starting to build in your communities. Yes, it is still tough for many of you, but you are starting to realise that there is no point stressing about that which you cannot change at this time. Make the most of your present circumstances. At another time you may look back fondly or with nostalgia at these times. Where is the still point within the chaos of ideas and apprehension? You are all getting to know yourselves a little better, for better or for worse. 'Know thyself' was the sacred motto at the oracle of Delphi. Those in families or couples are finding out about themselves through their relationships. Those alone are to a greater or lesser degree, re-defining their relationship with themselves. You are all realising your tipping points and your limitations, but be kind to yourself and others when they become apparent. Tolerance of self and others is needed now. Yes, be strong and resilient in your determination to move beyond this situation, but do not be rigid or inflexible in this undertaking. One day at a time is a gift that is yours to open.

Dear World

7th April

So, a gateway is open to another world. Becoming at one with universal harmony is a possibility to achieve for humanity and your earth plane existence. Do not be discouraged by the daily news hype. We are sending rays of light of many colours upon your world. The shadow is fading slowly but surely. Smile and be happy, you are allowed. It is not the destiny for all to suffer, though some may. Compassion is a healer in the long run. None really want another to suffer unless their mind or soul has been discoloured by another. Do not wait too long to be happy in what you do. There is time it is true, but engaging with the heart of life is rewarding when grabbed in both hands. There is always a shadow waiting to fall over you, but it cannot overcome your warmth of heart and generosity of spirit. Be the future you want to see.

Dear World

8th April

When all is said and done there is much to be said for patience. Time has ways of speeding up and slowing down, but when you long for the end of something it will always seem too slow. As we have said, bless each day and appreciate what it has to offer. What do we see in the future? The sun rises, a new day dawns. All things change, but some are faster than others and some need their time to happen. There is much questioning and discussing on this pandemic that is affecting you all. There is no one cause or solution, but many blessings becoming apparent in the pause it brings. In families, businesses, individuals and society, life is stripped back and afterwards many will question what now matters. For many that which seemed critical is now irrelevant and that which was last on the list comes to the fore. A soul or life stripped bare reveals much that was hidden. No longer worry about the end, but more the completion of the process.

Dear World

9th April

Signs of hope and good fortune are appearing around you. Take time to notice and be thankful for these, because they are indeed gifts. Paintings of rainbow children or pubescent birds of spring are messages of hope for shocked and tired souls. They have come to this world still fresh from realms of spirit and know the possibilities unfolding. They recognise and remember something in its unfolding that stirs a joy inside, though as yet unspoken. The seriousness of facts and figures of morbidity weigh heavy on the older ones, but recognition is enough. Sing a song of rainbows for those in need and it will be heard. That is our message now.

Dear World

10th April

Dear world we are worried about our future as pollinators of plants and vegetation on earth. Some are helping, some are not. We know you are. The chemicals that have been used and still are being used in many cases, effect deep into our genes, our hives and nests. Each generation is developing to survive rather than thrive. The world is a macrocosm of the microcosm that is our hive. Our communities suffer as yours do. People need to realise and farmers especially. It is not too late. We will do what we need to do, but humanity needs to change its priorities. There is little room for error now. An opportunity awaits mankind now to make things better for all life. It is time for the many to awaken to this, not just the few.

Dear World

11th April

So, there is so much noise, inner noise of your minds and outer noise of busy-ness and letting off steam. People have little regard for one another and their friends in nature in this respect. There may not be an easy answer. We do not want to spoil another's fun or industriousness and now you cannot walk away. These things are ideas for the future though. What is your ideal situation or home? There is much to be said for plans and dreams, even if they seem fruitless at this time. We know you think of your limitations in regards to resources, but if not explored, how will you know?

Dear World

12th April

So, Easter time is here, eggs and bunnies abound. Resurrection, rebirth and renewal is the theme. An idea not lost on you I hope. This year is an opportunity for all of this to happen. You are the embryo within the egg in your confinements, waiting to break out into the world. What world will you enter into? Is that your choice or someone else's? What lies beyond the horizon of your current vision? Rise up to see. Do not be held down by physical limitations. Be like the eagle and soar high to see beyond the mists that shroud the valleys of misfortune.

Dear World

13th April

So, another day dawns, we gather our resources and carry on with a stout heart and resolve. There seems to be a dilemma between carrying on and accepting each day for what it is and the call to do something more for those in pain and suffering. You need to start with yourself to get an understanding of what is happening and keep yourself in balance. Then you can work on others and the whole. Sometimes it is enough to feel and be the change in ourselves.

Dear World

14th April

So where are we in the curve of events affecting the earth? Somewhere in the middle of the intensity of infection it would seem. You are at a turning point it is true. Things may take a little while to catch up and be apparent. Slowly, slowly change in consciousness is occurring throughout the world, but the heaviness of change and its consequences cause distress of course. We know you are doing what you can. Sometimes to stand between heaven and earth and be the conduit of healing is all that you can do and it is well valued by us in spirit, because we too work for these aims. Allow yourselves to open up to a new beginning; it is your birth-right and destiny.

Dear World

15th April

So, what are these recurring pains and conditions that you feel from time to time? They never completely go away. Sometimes they act as a barometer of your soul in body. What are you overdoing? What is out of balance in your life? It cannot always be changed, but in spirit we love you and given time and space, will do all we can to heal you of these ailments. Of course, you need to do your part. Work with us in mind and body. Do not feel that you need carry these pains. They are not your cross to bear. It is ok to let go. You are allowed some joy and pleasure in your life.

Dear World

16th April

Peace from within begets peace without. The feeling that you are not enough or are not doing enough is very common in your society. You feel that much must be done before you die. Well maybe the promptings of spirit encourage this in some ways it is true, but there are also times to rest and ponder. Sometimes these can turn out to be the most productive in the long run. Take time to listen to others and yourself, for in this act peace will come.

Dear World

17th April

So, is it different now? What is happening around the world? The USA are dynamic, big steps one way then another, usually clumsily. Russia is secretive and sulky, making decisions behind closed doors and peeking out to look at other country's response. Europe is busy trying to be united in its differences and frustrated about its weaknesses. Britain is bold, resolute, but delusional in its promises. It has good intent, but ineptitude is not admitted to. Africa is used to disasters and illness, but lacks resources. Coming late to this they may benefit from the lessons and help of others. China is licking its wounds and slowly waking up, but fearing a backlash of opinion. South America is a continent of extremes in climate, geography and economics, this crisis will test its Christian principles. Australia and the south seas feel far away and they are tired of the onslaught, having to deal with the pandemic after gruelling fires is making them turn inward at their troubled soul. So, as you examine your own self so do nations, as the light of consciousness falls upon them.

Dear World

18th April

A little rain does you good my people. As plants perk up after a shower and bird song increases, so do the hearts of men. Water reminds us how to feel ourselves and step into the flow of life. After a period of sun and fire you need that breather. A raindrop is an interesting thing; a pearl of water containing a gift of life. Where you live in temperate lands the moods of weather are enshrined in your personalities and the character of your countries. Those of you who are using these times to be more observant notice these shifts in weather and mood. 'Raindrops Keep Falling on My Head' is a happy song that sums up the joy that rain can bring when needed. Do not be sad at these times. There is much to see, do and behold. You may not recognise yesterday's self for much longer. Blessed are the lonely ones, for they are understanding.

Dear World

19th April

It is good to see people outdoors in healthy pursuits, those that can. They are making time for a new normal that hopefully will continue long after this current crisis. This is one of our aims. Often too much business and unnecessary chores make the simple pleasures and family bonding fall by the wayside. There is much time now for healthier and happier lives for those that choose this path. There will always be those too ill, too old or too stubborn, but that is their choice or destiny. We can help and encourage, but ultimately time will tell. This joy in the simple outdoor life is settling the earth energy and embedding the new normal into place. Those that know and walk this path are beginning to feel it.

Dear World

20th April

Sometimes we are between a rock and a hard place. You are ok where you are but do not know where to go next. Choices are not easy at any time and even harder when you maybe not doing the choosing. At times it is ok to wait, but sometimes he who waits loses the prize. Ultimately, we know you keep your focus on the bigger work, but the desire for companionship and someone to share and understand your world is strong. At this time of year as spring awakens, these feelings are at their strongest. We are never alone of course, but as these times have shown all too clearly, human to human bonding is a wonderful gift. Always be open to the possibility without undue obsession over its outcome.

Dear World

21st April

You have seen many things in vision and life. It is all coming together and beginning to make some sense. We are watching over you, but not controlling you. The world is awakening and you are all co-creators. You are all making choices about what kind of world you would like to live in, both individually and collectively. When choices are made and the impulse is started we can help. Not everything is easy. There is some letting go and some holding on. What remains is what is left to grow and develop.

Dear World

22nd April

It is indeed a re-birth as you feel it to be. The earth mother has been incubating and is now re-birthing. She needed this still time to complete the process without harm. Of course, as the earth re-births into a new phase, so does all upon it. The long-awaited Aquarian age is upon us. Different parameters and desires are coming into reality. As you have been doing, it helps if you tune into this new vibration of life and assist in bringing it into existence. This will help yourself and the whole. People are still learning how to create this new world, so you still need to be understanding of each other. Be the beacon of light on the hill that guides others out of the darkness.

Dear World

23rd April

Nature is a wonder to behold and observing it is a blessing. This is the first level of communication. Feeling nature in all its manifestations is the second level of understanding. Merging with nature is the third level of being. When you begin to feel this connection and truth you are on the way to a greater understanding of life and indeed yourself. It is not for everybody to find this homeostasis, but these times are giving more inhabitants of earth the chance to reflect on this and possibly experience it. When you realise this connection with all of nature and life, many human practices become abhorrent to you. It is but one step further to realise the oneness in spirit, the supernatural and the universe beyond. When this realisation is absorbed into your being, then you realise that any abuse or imbalance in one part of the universe is felt by the whole.

Dear World

24th April

Every day we walk with you upon the earth. We see your efforts of healing this situation and world. We feel your heaviness of heart and weariness of mind. We see your invisible tears. There is nothing that we cannot do together to aid the healing, but you know it has to all come together. Be present in your dreams that are becoming, do not resign too easily. These are the most special of times and yet the most challenging. If you have been chosen, then you are up to it. Now rest a while. Today is done.

Dear World

25th April

It is written long ago that things will come to pass on earth that cause a reckoning, a questioning and a shake-up of all that is 'normal'. In different cultures and religions the symbols and metaphors may be different, but the meaning is the same. You all need to remember it is not a punishment, but a re-setting of impulse and direction as has happened over millennia at different times before. Yes, it will be viewed as necessary in hindsight, because of the inevitable overrun of the previous impulse. Accept that it has to come and it will come. Embrace and feel the positive wave of energy and ride with it. Look out for others, but do not be pulled down by those unseeing.

Dear World

26th April

What world lies beyond all this pain and suffering? You ask. It is yet to be known in many ways, but the ship is being held on a steady course now. The worst of the storm has passed, but it is not time to be complacent. There is damage to be repaired and dead to bury. Beyond all this are pleasant skies and healing hearts. The joy of reunion and human fellowship is not too far away. Then it will be time to clear up the debris and rebuild a future fit for all beings. Be at one with all, atonement.

Dear World

27th April

It is for all of us and you to find your place in the world. It is tempting to follow the crowd for the sake of belonging, but keeping to your own inner guidance is the only sure way. The collective that forms around you mirrors different parts of your projections into the immediate world around you. So that may be a comfort, though at times reveal uncomfortable truths about yourself. This is ok. It is how the soul grows. You may outgrow some and encounter new mirrors as you develop through life or pass through different stages. The hope is that all grow together, for in this there is much comfort and companionship to be had.

Dear World

28th April

Onward, onward we go with the wind behind us and a stout heart. We carry what we need and no more. We have reached the foothills and pause to gather our resources and rest a little. You are all stronger than you were before. Many of you have surprised yourselves with your resilience and ingenuity. Once given or realised, it is there for ever to be utilized when needed. There is still some climbing to be done, but you are well able and looking forward to the challenge. Do not be sad anymore. Life lies before you.

Dear World

29th April

We are here today to tell you about moving on from this current health crisis. There is a lot of talk about what changes are needed as well as risks of re-infection. There is yet to be a definitive guide to this process, but it will not take as long as some are suggesting. The bigger societal and economic changes are already happening because of the impact of the crisis. Moving forward these will be adapted in real time to deliver what is desired and demanded in the new world. Economically there will obviously be some short-term loss and change, but new opportunities and investments will appear that are more in line with the world desired by all. This will become like a snowball gathering momentum downhill. Where you individually place yourself in this situation is for all to decide, within their own framework of opportunity as given at the time. We are supporting and watching over this process.

Dear World

30th April

So, it is nearly May Day, a time for joyous celebration, a celebration of love, life and vigorous growth. It is still there even if your own movements are somewhat curtailed. You can see it all around you if you look outside and feel it within you, if you allow the feelings to arise. We are saddened by the lack of celebration this year, but it will be expressed in some way we are sure. When there is so much death and fear in the world is not life most ready to be celebrated. Be happy for its gifts and vow to share them when and how you can. The sun is in your heart and fire in your belly, let it cleanse and regenerate your soul and body. Welcome summer, vitality returns. All will be healed in its time.

Dear World

1st May

So, it is May Day, funnily that is also a distress signal. You all so much want to celebrate like you should and let it all go for a while, but the restrictions around you have become engrained. The Beltane fires would feel more like distress beacons if lit right now. Appropriate action and consideration for other's feelings, reflects a mature process and is desirable at times like these. Private celebration might be the order of the day. Collective healing and path-working are hard to co-ordinate when all are so far apart. Instead feel the love inside of you radiating outwards into the world around.

Dear World

2nd May

'Heaven' can be created here on earth, that is a heavenly way of being. More peaceful, understanding and living in harmony with all life. These things seem like dreams and illusions to many of you, but look at what has already begun to change. You just need the desire and endurance to keep going. Many eyes are opening and hearts as well. Believe in what you are doing, keep making that connection and allowing it to happen. The flow of life is beginning again. You are loved and cared for. The rainbow children are awakening.

Dear World

3rd May

There is much to be said for letting yourself go a little bit and having some fun. It is healing to the soul to move beyond your usual rigid framework of expression. It is even more important during these times of prolonged restriction. Sharing this with others is an added bonus, as it gives them permission to do the same. By that we mean free the spirit in some way. It also opens up the creative faculties and makes you smile. Do not be afraid to embarrass yourself now and then. You will be loved more for it and listened to more warmly.

Dear World

4th May

We watch upon you, all of you, from here in spirit. We applaud the way most of you have modified your ways in this crisis. You are looking well on it we think. Some suffer of course, but you are learning to accept other possibilities. Much is given and received in love and mutual understanding. The rose of love is yours. We understand on this threshold of change that apprehension is around you. We offer our protection and guidance to all who listen. A new world is unfolding, better than any you have known. Be patient our children and be with us on this journey. There is much yet to behold.

Dear World

5th May

So, let us talk about money, the financial world and how it might be changing. There are new opportunities for ethical investment as old ones fade away. Although pensions and other incomes are temporarily unstable, this will iron out. Money is a token of exchange of energy at some level, so it will always be apparent in some form. Just now it may be better to play the waiting game until things settle into a clearer perspective. The world as a whole is looking deep into how it functions, but it has to maintain services and function while it changes. It is ok to think about money and make prudent choices. Having enough and a little more is an admirable aim. In stability there are more options for service and love.

Dear World

6th May

There are different paces of recovery in each country of the world. This is according to their actions it is true, but also their individual karma as a nation and the make-up of their population. In the overall plan of enlightment and consciousness change we require an understanding of the world situation and a willingness to embrace necessary change or action. This happens through existing awareness of some and through awakening through trauma, which in this case is mainly the virus and its impact upon all. This enforced retreat of many citizens of earth has given them time to realise what is and is not important in life on this planet. Of course, not all reach the required level of realisation, but when enough are ready to influence the desired change and co-operation, healing begins. We ask this of you all, that no more are harmed.

Dear World

7th May

Here we are again on a full moon and quite a powerful one. The queen of the night and all that is hidden, the illuminator of thoughts and dreams and awakener of hidden desires. She is the governor of tides and stimulator of growth. Sometimes when the moon is full you can feel her light and energy in your third eye. What does this one mean? That which has been most hidden is at its most exposed state. What you see is what you get. There is less ability for others to mislead or distort truth. A full moon is always a time of emotionally heightened feeling and this is no exception. Focus on what is most true and relevant to you at this time. Feel the blessings of the moon mother goddess upon you. Feel the power of heart and mind as one.

Dear World

8th May

So today many celebrate the anniversary of victory in Europe, but is there ever really victory in anything? Where we see things there is only a cessation of conflict, on the surface at least. Sometimes the idea of a battle motivates action in some, but no enemy is ever purely that. The 'enemy' always represents something in ourselves waiting to be revealed or absorbed. This is true in respect of nations as well. The personality of a nation can be flawed and need new influences or challenges. Sometimes the enemy can be the bringer of, or at least the catalyst for change. This is also true in relation to the whole planet earth and humanity's role upon it. The current enemy, this virus, is but a bringer of change, a catalyst for the forming of new character and presence. We should give thanks for the sacrifices of the way-showers, but is victory not just acceptance of the new, or re-affirmation of life returned.

Dear World

9th May

Love is a beautiful thing and much desired. You crave to soften the hard shell around you and seek the love of another to help in this. The merging of two beings can melt the illusion of control that feels like the authentic you. The inner you needs to be known and shown and love holds the key to open the door to its expression.

Dear World

10th May

Love can connect us to all levels of being. It is a universal language that all beings of right mind understand. It is also the energy of transmission in its highest form, light of the heart magnified. When you raise your consciousness and journey to other levels of being, you can communicate through the mind, but the language of universal love transmitted from your spiritual heart is the purist form of interaction. It reveals the most profound healing and truest intent. This is not just idealistic speech or spiritual platitude. It is a universal rule apparent on earth as much as anywhere. We are never far from you in love.

Dear World

11th May

How are the children feeling now in all this? They have needed to adapt to a difficult situation quite rapidly and learn about some mature issues. For some there has been the benefit of the added security of quality time with their parents. Those lucky enough to have gardens or outside space have still had the benefit of sunshine, fresh air and exercise, but some are not so lucky. Those deprived in this situation are more likely to be those deprived before it began, sadly. This is another short-coming of your society needing to be addressed. Most children are resilient and adaptable and they will gain an appreciation for the more simple things in life. When they do meet up with their wider family they will love and appreciate them all the more. They may however fear the separation returning and these anxieties need to be considered. At an intuitive level they may understand more than you give them credit for. We are never truly separated from those we love.

Dear World

12th May

So, meeting up again after this time could be emotional. It has been a while and you are not sure how much you or the others have changed through this experience. Many of you have also become used to your solitary existence. You have developed ways to cope and even thrive. Breaking back out of this may challenge the framework you have built into your daily routine. It does need to be done though, one step at a time. Humans are social creatures by nature and do need some direct interaction to shape and form their own existence and development. We are watching over you as always. Visualise this process as if you are a flower slowly re-opening in the morning sun. It is an unfolding.

Dear World

13th May

We are waiting for a sign that things are different and have begun to change in the right direction. There has been an inner shift amongst many people, but we think there needs to be more. The world is beginning to wake up and return to work. In this process many will be faced with what they can or cannot tolerate any longer. We are shining a light on these things as many on earth now do themselves. Some carry on as before, which may be ok depending on their previous path. It is no longer acceptable to not consider the effect of your individual behaviour on the whole. Whether they be little steps or large strides, your actions make a difference. There is never a perfect time to reveal your truth, but this time is as good as any.

Dear World

14th May

So, let us get going if we can. The principle of movement is that the first step is always the hardest. This is true in a physical endeavour, but also true for a new project, idea or spiritual journey. We are always waiting to get on board with these movements. Finding the right means of expression and places or people to share it with can be tricky of course, but we share your desire to get it right. Walk with surety and a confidence in what lies behind the words, for is that not what you believe? We are waiting for the followers to arrive and when they do, we can begin. Many are in need of a new voice or to hear their own. Do not be sad, nothing is lost, only reborn anew. Everything happens for a reason, even if you do not know why. We take our leave and bless you in this work.

Dear World

15th May

The gardener understands the seasons and the rhythm of nature, for he is always observing. He needs to know when to plant and sow for the best and when to harvest. With experience he develops a sixth sense for these things and becomes more aware of the subtle changes each year. This is also true of human gardeners, those who nurture the growth of a human soul. They know the changing seasons that make up a lifetime and they get to know the subtle or greater changes that can happen in any year. They know how bad 'weather' or conditions may affect the growth of your soul and therefore try to guide and protect you from the worst storms. Your gardeners are your spirit guides and though they guide and protect you they also give you room to grow. As you mature spiritually you become aware of this process in others as well as yourself. As you are being tended you are all taking care of the great garden of life.

Dear World

16th May

The silent days are a blessing to behold. Sometimes the peace is around you and you still feel like you should be doing. We are not here to judge you, but to allow you to fulfil your potential. It is ok to have a quiet day and consider your next move. In a changing world you are making changes to your plans constantly and sometimes feel that it is hardly worth making any at all. Walking wildly through the chaos is not really an option any more for those with awareness. Consideration is never a negative trait, but of course it can lead to inertia. We are watching over the situation around you and looking for openings to appear. Man-made rules have a purpose, but can also be a hindrance. You are feeling your way through and that usually holds you in good stead.

Dear World

17th May

Liminal spaces and times serve as a gateway between worlds and realms of being. Sunrises, sunsets and eclipses are gateways between dark and light, our conscious and unconscious worlds. Shorelines stand at the threshold between earth and water, between our physical and emotional self. When you spend time there you become aware of the emotional depths that lie beyond and the physical certainties that are behind you. At the edge between, you glimpse something of the truer reality that lies between. Your sensitivity may awaken enough to be aware of the otherworldly beings and forces that inhabit these edge places. When you do spiritual work or seek guidance, you are standing at these thresholds in metaphor if not in a physical sense and if you do both together with open heart and mind; then much may be revealed and received by those who come in peace and with generous intent.

Dear World

18th May

Tears lie just behind the mask of contentment and understanding. Some past hurt or heart felt empathy is enough to encourage the flow. This is the pain and hurt of self and others stored away because there was no time and space to allow expression. Well now there is and it is ok to allow yourself to do so. Whether love lost, being misunderstood or the regrets of words unsaid and opportunities untaken, the pain is the same. Many times have we watched the furrowed brow and clenched fists of repression mask the unexpressed emotional fire inside. It is all too common and of course generally desirable in civil society, but if you can marry truth, integrity and passion when needed, it may save many hidden wounds.

Dear World

19th May

What is friendship? There are many ways in which people can have friendship. There are the full on, spending every spare minute together sort of friendships. There are the childhood friends that stay close forever. There are also the soulmates who understand without words and know how little or how much contact you need. Those who you know through shared activities and interests that may grow into something deeper. There are also those who drift in and out of your life as the years go by. Some people need many, some only a few. Take care of the friends that warm and lift up your heart, for they are a precious gift indeed.

Dear World

20th May

You ask, what are we doing with all this, this communication? Is there an end in itself, or are we all on a journey together, staying in radio contact while lost at sea? We are here to teach and guide and give a glimpse of a bigger picture and what possibilities may lie beyond your current horizons. Nothing is easy in earthly life, especially when you choose to stand at thresholds and open doors. This takes some courage and bravery for the sensitive souls needed to walk this path. Do not be shy in your expression of truth that we share with you. Not everyone is awake and ready. Keep sharing when you can and remember what can be. Do not be frightened, as we have your back. Technology is just a tool to use and master; it is not an end in itself.

Dear World

21ˢᵗ May

A threshold of understanding lies before us all. There is a way in which you can open yourself to this through being in a state of receptivity and calm. Let go of negative thoughts that block this progress. There is a concept that you need to understand in which some of the old rules no longer apply. This means that which you feel may have failed before will not necessarily meet the same ends now. You may find your approach is on a different level of understanding and therefore throw up different results. It may take some practice to adjust to this difference, but it will be rewarding if you can. There is always an apparent window of opportunity that is ready and waiting to be opened. Do not think there is only one and you have missed it. Fear of failure is a common trait and understandable, but take courage and move beyond it. There is never a time more pregnant with possibilities than this one. We are with you on this.

Dear World

22nd May

We are with you on this undertaking. Many are awakening to new possibilities around them. Thinking creatively is exciting and unsettling in equal measure. The current restrictions have highlighted all restrictions in your life and psyche. Old patterns are breaking down to make way for the new. There is much to be said for 'fortune favouring the brave' at this time. Consideration for others is paramount, but it is ok to expect success in your endeavours. We are waiting to support those who come with good intent. There is nothing wrong with an entrepreneurial spirit if it is engaged towards building stepping-stones towards a better world. There is more to be said and more to be done. The eagle soars high now and takes in all that lies below.

Dear World

23rd May

So, there has been a move forward in this work. New portals have been opened. There is much need at these times and a hunger to learn and understand. Do not be afraid of what is to come and the demands put upon you. Everything can be managed. We thank you all for your openness and acceptance into this process. Nothing we say to you is without reason and consideration of its effect. You are all finding your way through the forest and we wish for you to enjoy the process of learning and renewal. The joy of future possibility is within your grasp.

Dear World

24th May

So where are we now in world terms? Are there still clouds of despondency and despair, or songs of hope and joy? Of course, there is yin and yang, but the outward turn of the spiral has begun, for most at least. The earth itself has examined its own inner core as you have yourselves. Coming out of that contracted state is not easy. There is hesitating and caution, which is valid. There is no rush, each in their own time. Like sleeping beauty, you awaken from your slumbers and dreams, unsure what is real anymore. Stretch and breathe deeply. Morning has broken.

Dear World

25th May

Social distancing is a strange phrase that has come into use in this current crisis. Humans are social animals, yet you are being called upon to act against your nature. There are of course many reasons given for this practice, but it is causing a sickness of soul deeper than that which it is meant to prevent. Children feel it and adults too. We are not here to judge the actions of your leaders, for they have difficult decisions to make, but let us hope the separation does not go on any longer than is prudent. We can hope at least that it will make all appreciate the blessing of human bonds and contact as you move beyond this period. Of course, we in spirit may seem distant to you and in some ways we are, but in these quiet times we hope you have found us nearer to hand and heart.

Dear World

26th May

So, there is a feeling among some of you that it is all over regarding this crisis. This is not so. Although things have moved along there is still much below the surface to be revealed. The changing face of humanity belies the unspoken truth, which needs to be heard. There are still too many shadows in the halls of power and an 'I scratch your back, you scratch mine' attitude. Transparency engenders trust and without trust there cannot be progress in this respect. The thought forms that come from hidden motives are the same that lead to mass pandemic. It is not just on the physical level, but poison to the mind that needs to be healed. It will be done, but takes the hearts and minds of all to make it happen. We are with you in this endeavour.

Dear World

27th May

The young ones have much to teach us. They understand more about this new world than the adults. They were born with its blueprint in their destinies. They are suffering much in these times of restriction, but in their soul's they realise that it is a necessary part of a bigger plan. The unfolding of their dreams of a better world begins with the realisation of its possibility. There is much unsaid, but the signs are there. Listen closely and follow their lead.

Dear World

28th May

So, there is a feeling among the masses that all is not as it should be. That means that they think there is something they are not being told. This is not necessarily true. It is more that those in power have much before them that they do not know the outcome of. Rather than being honest about this, they create shadows that ordinary people view with suspicion. Things will gradually change in this respect we believe. Honesty is the best policy. If more people take time to sit and meditate, they will understand the deeper truth and nature of things for themselves and will be less swayed by rumour and hearsay. Honest appraisal of an individual's actions and motivations is always valid, but do not judge with anger.

Dear World

29th May

Don't look back in anger, we say to you. The past is what it is, the past. You have the choice to choose how you relate to it. Yes, it has shaped your choices and destinies, but the individual factors in your past are the kerbstones that have kept you on the road where you now find yourself. You have choices now. Life might not be ideal for some, but blaming the past will not resolve it. Be thankful for the blessings you do have, then they will multiply. Do not worry too much about the detail. Believe things will be better and they will. We know we warn you against misfortune at times, but these coming times are opportunistic in outlook, if approached with good intent. Do not overthink, but be open to the unfolding story of life.

Dear World

30th May

As you all begin to return to the outer world, it seems exciting, but also noisy and tiring to the senses. You are torn between loving the return of social interaction and missing the solitude of individual contemplation. In some ways, that which has gone within is peering out into the world and feeling how it has changed, if at all. Do not be surprised by how you feel and who you encounter. It is all an expression of the inner-you revealed. We are what we believe, some say. Let us slowly awaken from the slumber and observe ourselves. It is ok to be happy in the company of others. Each will find their own pace. The chrysalis opens when the butterfly is ready to spread its wings.

Dear World

31st May

Enchantments of the soul occur when human and faerie realms interact. This is when an increased perception of the possibility of that world awakens the imagination. Although imagination is needed to open the doorway, what is perceived or felt is not just imagined. When you become close to nature, with nature, then all the energies that govern its complex interaction become apparent to you and in that moment you become apparent to them. If you are lucky enough to enter that world with beneficial intent, only good will follow from it, but you will be increasingly saddened by those with an uncaring attitude to life, nature and the earth.

Dear World

1st June

The time has come to open our hearts and be honest with ourselves and others. There is much to be said for keeping our inner selves hidden and secret, but if you want to be truly known and to know and help others, then be open to reveal what is inside. This is part of a bigger process regarding mental health for all and it takes some courage. So, begin with those you trust the most. What we are saying, is that for the health of nations and the whole of humanity, do not lie to yourself about what you are feeling. In that way you begin to open the dialogue for others.

Dear World

2nd June

Silence is golden, but hard to find in your modern, crowded world. Some people cannot stand the silence. They are scared they might have to listen to their own voice. Others crave it, to hear their inner voice, accompanied only by the sounds of nature. We should not judge the uninitiated or frightened ones. They may have been children haunted by nightmares and fear the depths of their own thinking. Pray for them and be thankful for your own peace when you find it. Use it wisely. Do not be disturbed by that which is not yours to carry. Send peace, love and the light of conscious understanding to where it is needed. For in this we stand with you. It is not in vain.

Dear World

3rd June

Travel can open the mind and senses if undertaken with the right attitude. You do not always have to go too far either. Being open to new experiences and discoveries is good for the soul and engenders a more positive attitude to different people and cultures. Travel is difficult at these times still, but what is rationed needs to be used wisely and will be more appreciated when it is experienced. The excitement of exploring and discovering somewhere new awakens something within. It need not be a far-off land; it may be an unexplored footpath or lane close to home. There are some risks still, but they will reduce in time. Care for the planet and countryside is foremost, but those who have witnessed its beauty and diversity become the greatest ambassadors for its love and protection. Nothing is forbidden in this respect. None of you travel without consideration of its impact, or without joy for the blessings it reveals.

Dear World

4th June

So, there are many things we still have need to speak about, although much has been covered. You know little of the spiritual dimensions and how they influence the earthly realms. Yes, you may perceive our influence, but you understand little of the means of our application of spiritual or divine will. It is always a matter of conjecture regarding free will and divine influence or fate. Both operate on earth of course, but the proportion varies according to the individual and the prevailing circumstances. Some choices that individuals make are of little consequence to the path of their soul, but if they are moving too far from their soul potential in this lifetime or are failing to resolve karmic issues, then spirit may intervene.

There is also a collective responsibility and destiny, which has become quite apparent during these recent times. Spiritual intervention is indeed working through these adaptions, trying to minimise pain and hurt, but allowing human and planetary evolution to come to fruition. You can still exhibit some free will, but some of the governmental restrictions are a reflection of spiritual ones that allow a pause for change and healing to occur. It may not be enough. There is much coming to the surface still. We are always indebted to your service.

Dear World

5th June

Beyond the moon lies unexpressed sorrow. There is much unsaid and held within, waiting for the right time to let go. The full brightness of the moon blinds us to what lies beyond. An eclipse shades that brightness if only for a while, then the true emotion can be revealed or expressed. Be gentle in what you see in yourself and others at this time. It may be a surprise to all. Do not be saddened too much by what you feel. It will pass away in time. Feelings always do.

Dear World

6th June

There is much to be said for watching and waiting when your thoughts are misty. If you all have learned anything during this time of lockdown it should be that you do not need to be constantly moving forward. There are times to consider, contemplate or relax. We are with you at these times of change within a year of change. Breathe deep, enjoy the moments that you can and feel where life is calling you.

Dear World

7th June

Ancestors of yours inhabit different planes on the spiritual realms to that of guides generally. They are aware of your earthly connections regarding family, places and interests. As when they were alive on earth, they are concerned with your well-being and that of your whole family group. There is sometimes a balance to be sought between the guides who encourage progress on the spiritual path and ancestors who wish to see your familiar happiness and well-being. What you would recognise as the goddess forces work to oversee this balance. At these times, this nurturing aspect is returning more to the fore, because it is essential in understanding the new dynamic. Sometimes ancestral spirits newly born to this realm need to understand the higher spiritual ideals at play and this can take some time. We are all looking after your best interests and that of the whole.

Dear World

8th June

So, we begin the unwinding. A thread has been wound across your lives over the centuries, that holds you all in its grasp like a spider's web. It has been around for so long that most have become unaware of its entanglements. So why the unwinding you ask? The release of old patterns that no longer serve is necessary, if jarring in its manifestation. Once free from these threads new ones can be wound, more fitting for the new societies and visions of future harmonics that are being birthed. The midwives of nations, societies and races should hold steady and true during these unfolding times. Know your roles and play them well, for everyone matters now.

Dear World

9th June

Asceticism and the denial of feelings and desires is a long and established means of withdrawing from society in order to try and obtain spiritual connection and enlightenment. Very few have the discipline and opportunity to carry it out to its full extent, but it is not for everyone to walk this path anyway. Engagement with the world is also important in spiritual unfoldment and inner discovery. You have all undertaken a period of confinement and reduction in outer distractions and most will have felt some benefits from this in their own being and maybe with those around them. We cannot all be hermits though and engagement with the world is desirable and necessary for most. It is our hope and belief that this incubatory period has brought inner changes that will become realised as you all gradually return to your outer lives.

Dear World

10th June

Is it then not a very human trait to feel strong emotions at times? Be that from hurt to anger, to guilt, to tears of sorrow or love. It may be yours alone and go as quickly as it came, or come from long forgotten wounds now exposed. The injustices of the less fortunate, be they human or other creature, can release passions in your soul. So where to go with the pain and hurt of an unjust world? Work to your strengths to correct wrong-doings, but also admit your own. Never create more harm or hurt than that which you endeavour to prevent or correct. Ultimately it is for those beyond you to make these judgements.

Dear World

11th June

So here we are again, caught between heaven and earth observing what could be and what is, in equal measure. In many ways it feels like the hardest point in this process. You feel it could go either way; slip back to the unjust and economically battered, earth ravaging ways; or open-up to possibilities of co-operation, innovation, sustainability and justice of opportunity that have appeared in your visions. Remember to acknowledge the former, but give your energies to the latter. It is not by chance that changes are made, but by united and inspired co-operation and understanding. We are aware of scars being opened and angry wounds revealed. Compassion is needed, but hold onto the stillness at the centre of the storm.

Dear World

12th June

There is much to be said for working with the hands and doing practical things. It allows the mind to rest on the task in hand and pause its persistent worrying. Some practical problem solving and honest achievement satisfies the soul and encourages relaxation. Some people of course take this to extremes and never stop in their tasks, but all should spend some of their day or week in this manner if they are able. It is also very grounding to remember that physically working with the hands produces physical results. It is also comforting to have a little bit of life that you can shape to your own plan. We do of course encourage you to reach for the heights, but you need also to bring it all back home and earth.

Dear World

13th June

There is always something that needs to be said regarding the nature of a situation, or to bring knowledge and wisdom. Words may not always come easily, but they are there. Sometimes it helps to feel the flow of the words as they stream forth. Let a trickle become a stream, then a river. Sometimes silence is the best support, but many of you fear saying the wrong thing, so say nothing. You may also feel you do not have the authority or knowledge to share your opinion. If you consider your feelings and reaction to something, then you are free to express it with due care and consideration, or to remain silent. The dominance of a strong personality or opinion can render many speechless. It can take many years to find your own voice. When you do, be happy and encouraging to those yet to find their own.

Dear World

14th June

It is not for everyone to be heroes and villains. Some are way-showers, healers or peace-makers. No argument is black and white, though it may appear to be. There is some pain in all our ancestry; some is more recent than others. It is not for you to re-write history, but it is the time to write tomorrow's history. We are not saying everything is perfect or is going to be, but what do you really want the legacy of these times to be for your children and grandchildren. It is not all about anger, for anger breeds anger. It is love that matters, for in love there is unity.

Dear World

15th June

We speak for the ancestors at these times. Though your boat may be tossed around on the waves of a changing world, we are the anchor holding you steady in the storm. There is much happening that we do not understand, though we are given enough to realise the necessity. We do still care for your welfare and try and help in this and give you energy from below and stand behind you. Even the eagle needs a stable home to rest in. Much has been said about what is new, but it needs to be grounded in the world of familiarity that surrounds you.

Dear World

16th June

Three years have passed since the beginning of this cycle of events and in three more it will be complete. From the trough of a wave to the peak and down again; even what seem to be random events are part of waves and cycles. That is the way of nature, even when events appear to be beyond a natural cause. Even the epochs of time occur in cycles and waves of impulse. The acts of man may appear to be out of synch with these patterns, but overall he is still following those rhythms. The events of this year may have reminded many how they have little choice but to follow these chains of events. You are not powerless, but you need to direct your influence wisely and allowing for the greater patterns and flows of life that are playing out.

Dear World

17th June

So today we talk about life and death and the bridge that connects the two. You are not alone in wondering how the transition happens. In a natural death the soul has knowledge that the time of passing is approaching. They may have dreams that tell them so, or see family in spirit. Depending on their beliefs and readiness, they may be accepting of this passing or fight it. On passing from their body they may stay close to familiar people and places until their funeral or other letting go. It is in these early times of passing that family may be aware of their presence. Some people take a while to realise they have gone, especially if their death was sudden or traumatic. This is when spiritual help from you on the earth plane and us in spirit helps these souls come to terms with this and to begin moving on and to heal their soul. We are not judging on anyone on passing, but it is for them to assess their own life.

Dear World

18th June

You are loved and protected. Although you may feel at times that no one understands you or ever will, it is not the case. No two people on earth have the same understanding and outlook. You all have uniqueness and individuality. This is the beauty of human existence and also its strength. So, do not be saddened by your unique traits and way of looking at the world. You will always find people who share part of your view and may well love you for the part that they do not quite understand. Celebrate and enjoy these gifts in yourself and others, for in them exists the seed of creation.

Dear World

19th June

You are never alone if you are dedicated to your path and take time to connect to the indwelling spirits that surround you. There are many that are ancient and primal in nature, but certainly not primitive. Their sensibilities are greater than ours and they feel our needs and pain. The relationship is an empathetic one, built on trust and a shared desire to move towards natural and human healing. Do not shy away from or doubt these encounters, for they are as real as your human ones and more. They awaken a remembrance and return to a level of being that understands real connection between all beings.

Dear World

20th June

So here we are, the longest day is upon us and what have you done in this time of maximum growth and restriction. A contrary dynamic producing an unnatural tension in the soul, but not unlike initiatory methods used in ancient mystery schools in order to awaken perceptions and reduce distractions. Much of what has grown for you may not be immediately obvious to outsiders. The gifts may be within or moulded into your character. Let us welcome this time of maximum outer light and hold the memory within. For some it never came and you do well to give thanks for deliverance and pause to give blessings to those who have moved beyond the veil.

Dear World

21st June

So, let us talk about the coming times, an awakening. We know some of you see things starting to look like they are going back to normal and maybe that is a mixed blessing if there is no change for the better. A second wave may not happen in terms of the virus, but further waves of spiritual impulse will occur in some way. It is not for us to determine their means of expression on earth, but to hold the energy and open gateways of perception and light. Each in their own time; maybe you were already there. Enjoy what you have right now, it is always a blessing.

Dear World

22nd June

There is always more to be said of love and the way that it can move mountains at times. This is especially true in the collective sense when applied to situations or institutions that need that impetus to find a new way of being. This means that if you work from your heart centres in creating, praying, campaigning or in sending healing to a situation, then what is born of that will emanate from that heart centre itself. This may seem obvious to you, but often people see injustices and use anger to fuel their desire to create something better. If this happens to you, move towards love, because it needs to be at the centre of the new beginning you seek. You are sowing seeds of love, not breaking down walls.

Dear World

23rd June

There are new possibilities on the horizon. New encounters or the renewal of old ones are possible. There are still parts to play in this unfolding story. Let the dust settle and see who is around you. More is to be revealed. Understanding yourself is crucial in realising your strengths and gifts, but also in knowing the help you need. Nothing happens by accident now. There are patterns in the apparent chaos. Keep on your daily path and notice what unfolds.

Dear World

24th June

Midsummer's day marks the turning point of the year, when the days from now on slowly begin to shorten. It was a day of feasting and celebration in the past and was to the summer as Christmas is to the winter. That is the feast day after the solstice. Although the days begin to shorten the heat in the land continues to build. You can feel that zenith point within and allow it to revitalise and feed the fire within, the spiritual fire. At the winter solstice and Christmas, it is the memory of this light and fire rekindled within that is reborn in the solar and spiritual cycle of the year.

Dear World

25th June

So today we are talking about the world as we see it. There is a lightness of spirit among many celebrating the joys of summer and this is as it should be. The dark shadows are fading now. The sun is cleansing of many things, but also carries some harmful rays. The world is pulsing to a new rhythm, which you need to listen to so you can dance along to this new beat. On your own or when you gather again, you need to dance, sing, chant or drum along to bring this vibration more into realisation. This we leave with you.

Dear World

26th June

The expectation of the masses is that they should be provided for by whatever means necessary. This may not seem an unreasonable assumption on the face of it, but even children have to learn the link between effort and reward, or right action and beneficial results. It is not that effort and reward are always directly quantifiable on the material plane, but at least there is some link. We are not judging anyone for needing a secure life and the main requirements for living, but it does a disservice to an individual if they are denied the opportunity to fulfil their potential through some of their own effort and skill.

Dear World

27th June

There is much to be said for a quiet life, but it is not the natural state for human life in the long run. As social beings you thrive on those interactions that shape the personality and the experiences of the personality shape the life of the soul. There is a time to meditate and ponder, to walk in silence and feel the god in nature, but also a time to share and recollect these experiences among others. If the results of the life of solitude and spiritual practice are not for the benefit of the whole, they become an indulgence and can lose their imminent meaning and power.

Dear World

28th June

So here we are again, between and betwixt. Doors are opening and some normality is returning, but how does it sit with you. Some of it feels fine depending on those whom you encounter. There is still caution and even fear in some. The inconsideration of a minority is even more apparent than before. A crisis highlights strengths and vulnerabilities, be it personal or societal and these times are no exception. The actions of those who care little for human life or the environment leave open wounds on the surface of the possibilities of a kinder, cleaner world that most are breathing into existence. Keep on keeping on. Do not be swayed from your endeavours.

Dear World

29th June

Sometimes it is ok to rest your mind from the toil of seeking understanding and to walk barefoot in the grassy young woodland. The profusion of vigorous silver birch signifies new beginnings and youthful enthusiasm. They are among the first to grow on barren or deserted land. Whatever your age, you need at times to refresh in this landscape of inner or outer rejuvenation for the haggard soul. Breathe the late spring air and listen to the birdsong and remember it is all but part of you.

Dear World

30th June

Six months have passed this year of all years. We are healing you as you allow yourselves to be healed. There is much pain to be released, both personal and collective. The letting go allows for moving on. As we step into the waning year you no longer need to hold your breath. Let it out and breathe in deeply. Allow the healing of spirit to wash over you. You have made it this far, so be happy for that. There is still much to be done, but the way will be a little easier from now on. Be kind to yourselves and others. Stop punishing yourselves with the misdemeanours of those that went before. We are with you now more than ever, so be blessed in this.

Dear World

1st July

Do not judge the world on the actions of a few unruly young people. There are many good, inspiring young people around the world who know the true way forward. Their energy and enthusiasm will come to light in the coming months, as they do not wish to be judged by the actions of the inconsiderate ones. When light of truth and opportunity meet, then miracles can happen. The wealth of creation and opportunity exists in all ages, so let those willing to undertake the new movement begin.

Dear World

2nd July

It is enough to be yourself and listen sometimes. It matters not what you call your god or goddess. There is a time for worship and praise, but not now. These times are about the collective effort of many in spirit, on earth, of many faiths and none, but who see and feel a future better than the recent past. The revealing of this possibility is not exclusive, but inclusive. Do not be shy or precious with your dreams for they are not yours alone. Open your eyes and see the shadows fading. There is more to be said, but enough for now.

Dear World

3rd July

The constant chatter and worry of the human mind is engaging, but a little frustrating to those trying to impress on that mind greater truths, or even healing. It is the nature of man to busy himself with this and that and reflect on things said and unsaid. You are afraid a little when it stops and you have to face the silence within. What hidden truth about yourself will be revealed? There is nothing to fear, for all is already known by soul. Bringing knowledge into realisation in this incarnation is a steady progress and not without hurdles to overcome. Be still in heart and mind and then the still small voice of spirit can be heard.

Dear World

4th July

Let us go walkabout. The aboriginal people of Australia have the right idea. When life feels a bit stuck or lacking flow, walk and explore in the outside world. This re-energises connection with place and spirit. Ancient tracks and pathways hold the memories of many passers-by. Human and creature encounters add colour to the journey and give clues to hidden messages. One journey or walk inspires another. The reward of deep sleep follows.

Dear World

5th July

You have to learn how to balance and manage the effects of other personalities reacting or engaging with your own. To sensitive types this can be a wondrous exchange, or sometimes confusing, even debilitating. This is why the entrance to the Oracle of Delphi had the message 'Know Thyself'. This is because in really knowing yourself you are not as susceptible to the expressions of another, be they living being or spirit. This knowing keeps you grounded and level-headed, allowing you to enjoy interaction and exchange of ideas without fearing absorption of your own self. It is important to still spend some time alone, especially after you have become used to it in recent times. Balance in all things, a sense of perspective and sense of humour will help greatly in this endeavour.

Dear World

6th July

So, let us have a heart to heart you and me. You are better than you think you are and more loved. Do not beat yourself up about minor things. Do you not try to be kind to others and take care of the world around you? Then why is it that you doubt that you are good enough? The society of perfectionism is damaging to the souls of the silent, kind ones and many others. Of course, you endeavour to do a task to the best of your ability, but the passage of life goes up and down and no one can be on top of everything all the time. You also learn more from mistakes and learn empathy for others in the process. Be satisfied with who you are. You are enough.

Dear World

7th July

What is it that makes each one different from another? Genes, yes for sure, but each has a racial, environmental and soul circumstance of birth. None of these are indicative of potential in life, but they do give a set of circumstances that will tend to give certain experiences, which in turn leads to certain lessons and therefore spiritual growth, it is hoped. Ultimately you all experience each circumstance, so that is why judgement of others background is a futile undertaking. It is how you deal and grow through these lives given to you that shape the uniqueness of your soul.

Dear World

8th July

So today is interesting in terms of the development of life on earth. New discoveries are being made around the world, though unknown to each other as yet. As these discoveries become known they will bring together a bigger picture of past knowledge and future potential regarding life on this planet. Ancient wisdom and emerging technology provide solutions to some current problems as yet unseen. There is always an unfolding narrative to the epic story of life on earth. As a new chapter begins, its conclusion is yet to be written.

Dear World

9th July

The daily tasks of life weigh soft or heavily on your being, depending on your mood and health. There is always something to be done it seems in the life of home and work. We know that you may often like to be doing something more exciting, inspiring or relevant, but day to day tasks and also weekly, monthly and yearly ones give pattern and stability to your lives. This is calming for the nerves and constitution and provides balance to the extraordinary events and experiences that punctuate the lives of many. A methodical and managed approach to what needs to be done benefits all in the long run.

Dear World

10th July

So how is it that worlds collide and then move on without looking back. This is the all too real metaphor that describes forces of different polarities that come together in order to work out the more balanced result that eventually follows. In life you may experience this as conflicting political or personal opinions. It sometimes results in wars or other upheaval. If we look at the image of two worlds colliding, it is apparent that for this to happen there must be a force of attraction in operation. This means that each realises that it needs something of the other at some level. The less traumatic way would be to find it inside itself first, then merging would be less dramatic, but the passage of life and universe does not always work this way unfortunately.

Dear World

11th July

There is something that needs to be said about the way that the young people of the world are seeing things. They do not see the world through the same eyes as the older generation and yes that has always been so, but they came into this world with a different agenda which may have been dormant initially, but now is very much awake. The young people identify with each other in some way regardless of race, nationality or gender. We are talking about the general impulse and tendency, not the mutations brought about by conditioning or bad experience. This is their main focus as it should be, but it is ok to remind young people of other issues and traditions that other generations find important. Just remember what their main impulse is and it will make it easier to understand their nature and motivation.

Dear World

12th July

Much has been said. Much water has passed under the bridge. There are things that you would like to hear and some you would not. This is the nature of human life. We could always tell you more, but we are discerning in allowing enough dissemination of knowledge to bring healing and growth. Too much revealed too soon negates your own efforts and exploration. You will find as you share knowledge with others you will know the right amount to share that they can absorb. As you are shown, so you pass onto others. This is the way of knowledge and true wisdom; unfolding the layers of truth within and without.

Dear World

13th July

Time for a change maybe. A new world order is forming. Although on the surface there is not much difference as it appears, below the surface there is movement. Yes, we repeat this message in different ways, but you all need constant reassurance that all is not in vain. Has all this been for nothing? You ask. That is why we are saying that no, it has not been in vain. A new understanding is emerging. There is less tolerance for deceit and abuse of power. Discernment in business and personal matters are more to the fore. Also, we see a better balance in home, work and leisure, as many have now experienced the benefits. This is not just a hope, but an observable reality. It is for everyone to partake in this life anew.

Dear World

14th July

We are beholden to ourselves in what we do. By this we mean our spiritual and earthly selves are contracted to each other ultimately to be as one, but to work in either plane to achieve the greatest benefit. By this we mean a fulfilling life, a conscious life, a warm life of heart and soul. There is never a better time to re-affirm this connection. In this we help to complete your earthly and spiritual mission. With this we are entrusted.

Dear World

15th July

Let us ask ourselves where we will be this time next year. What will be the same and what will be different? The good times and bad times may continue, but will you be different in how you respond and react, or is it all to be a familiar repetition of the present. We would hope that all will move on and choices will be easier. To be a little older and wiser is expected, but the theatre of expression may change its hue. Priorities are shaping and forming and doors opening and closing. Be steadfast and true in whatever you do.

Dear World

16th July

So enough is enough. It is about time this virus went away you all think, but how. It may be that there are forces that are working towards this. There are always others that are working the other way, but this is the nature of life. Lessons have been learnt. There has been suffering and new revelations of self and society. There is never so much hidden, yet close at hand; never so much given, yet unappreciated. The light of opportunity and blessing lays upon this land, but it needs to be taken hold of. The cycles of boom and bust are over. What unfolds now is born of shared experience and hope for renewal. Do not be deterred by initial failures, it is the long-term impetus that will win through now.

Dear World

17th July

As the seas erode the edges of our shores, spiritual waters erode the edges of our being. All is forever in flux, taken from one place and deposited in another. When you stand at the water's edge and feel the dynamic of this in-between world, you feel the power of tide and storm. You also feel the resistance of the land holding its ground, but occasionally yielding. This is a dynamic which lives within all beings; the liminal space between different elements and worlds. This is where the magic happens and spiritual synapsis fire across the divide. Be conscious and aware of this. Be playful, yet respectful. For in this manner good deeds are done.

Dear World

18th July

To live a life long and strong is not an easy undertaking. We are all susceptible to peaks and troughs, where everything seems so much effort. To keep a willing mind and willing body takes dedication, resilience and a strong spirit. You also need to learn the art of rest and withdrawal at times. Knowing how to pace oneself and sense when active periods are arising is desirable. Sometimes a little rest and recuperation before a demanding time is worth far more than attempting to recover afterwards. You may not always know what is around the corner, but maturity brings a sense of expectation for all eventualities that is often undervalued.

Dear World

19th July

There is time and love enough to go round, so do not fear the lack of it. There is no limit to the love that can pour forth from an individual and even more so from the spiritual source that feeds us all. Feel its abundance around you and within you. Breathe in love and breathe it out. There is never so much need to share that around. The quiet corners of our world hold lonely souls, so remember them at these times. There is always time, just do not be its slave. The hour of uncertainty is passing and time moves on. Love over time.

Dear World

20th July

Enough is enough regarding wanton waste and destruction on the planet. Those who have not a care for nature when they leave their mess behind are lost and sad souls indeed. It is not enough just to name and shame, it requires the resetting of their belief systems. It is incomprehensible to those who care for the environment and mother earth that some people litter and dump without remorse or guilt. Whosoever commits these crimes is undeserving of the care of her who cares for her own. Their plight is their own. Educate and encourage where you can, but some may be beyond the threshold of redemption. It saddens us as it does you, for they have not learned anything from this crisis. We stand with those who care.

Dear World

21st July

So, days and weeks pass and a new moon arises. The fortunes of man and beast are mixed and many in shape. Though the summer is at its height it seems all too short in front of you. Awaken yourselves in heart as you finally come together in spirit. There is time for thanksgiving and a little sorrow. What has changed and what remains of the still centre. Appreciate what you have, savour it and send it forth. There is a world in need and still in trauma. Strong and open are the gates to the garden of peace. Enter while you can and replenish at its healing spring of rejuvenation.

Dear World

22nd July

Nature blooms, nature remembers, nature forgets. The gifts that are given to you are deserved. Those who listen are listened to. Those who walk the careful path see the vision of life that is multi-faceted. A moment of true connection speaks a thousand words and reassures the wandering, wondering spiritual traveller that the path they walk is where they should be. Acknowledge the gift and blessing for what it is and carry on with a good heart.

Dear World

23rd July

The demands and pleasures of life awaken and you come to realise how much you have come to appreciate the quiet solitary times. The joy of interaction is honestly felt and wished for, but many have resolved not to lose that which has been gained. Life has a way of showing lessons through experience of excess and denial. We resolve to find the balance, but often fail. It is to be remembered that the art of balance requires the awareness of daily, weekly monthly and longer fluctuations and patterns of activity. Going with the flow is sometimes necessary in order to get back on the horse. Love what you have missed, now that you can.

Dear World

24th July

What is the silence in the noise, the unheard voice hidden behind the chaotic behaviour of unruly youth? Too much unexpressed and locked down inside comes out in peer driven explosions of rebellion and celebration, confused in their marriage of convenience. When all is said and done, it is said and done. Maybe your desired right is a rite, of passage as such. What now you children no more. Welcome to the evolving world of responsibility. Play your part well.

Dear World

25th July

So, who are we, the watchers and waiters that look upon you all and prod and poke your consciousness into action? We are what you have been and are yet to become. We are the sisters of your souls that feel the fire and hope giving birth before you. We are the ones who stand behind you when you doubt and lift you up when you fall. We are the words that come from nowhere when you fear their loss. We are the sons of father's pride fulfilling. We are the ones that see nature's dream unfolding, yet too bright to see. Given space and time we will unlock those dreams and fears that block the world renewing. This is who we are.

Dear World

26th July

There is a time and place where everyone feels at home; their déjà vu moment. They feel like they have been there before because they have. The soul remembers places and people to which it has had a strong bond. In this way the spirits of the land remember the passing of souls and especially those who acknowledged them in previous incarnations. In other words, if your soul had a spiritual relationship with a particular place, then if you re-encounter it, the depth of that connection will be re-awakened. Sometimes this leads to the remembering of other aspects of that life. These moments are not uncommon, but brushed aside by many. Treasure them when they happen and learn their lessons while the gateway is open to you.

Dear World

27th July

Honour and responsibility are admirable qualities that are missing from much of today's society. The ability and intent to stick to your word and that which you have promised is the responsible way to behave. There is little heed paid to these qualities in much of modern society, but it really is a matter of empathy. Do unto others as you would have done unto you. Honour your commitments or explain in good time why you cannot. It is the responsibility of all to care for each other, the world around us and respect the effort and time of others. Do not be put off by individuals who do not show these manners. Do not lessen your own standards. Maintain dignity and compassion in the delegation of your duties as much as you are able. In this you become honourable.

Dear World

28th July

There will always be some days that are harder than others. There may be no apparent rhyme or reason that is obvious to you, but this is how it is. Energy flows and pulses. The moods of earth and planets have their say and humanity reacts. Keeping your feet firmly on the ground at these times is important. Accept what is yours to change and reject what is not. Wait for the dust to settle on a new day and see what unfolds. Each feeling has its time. Good days also appear out of the blue, so accept them with the same grace and humility.

Dear World

29th July

Sometimes we try and get away from ourselves, but cannot. The desire is to get away from it all, but you find the thoughts go with you. A change of scenery or some distraction may help, but sooner or later the need is to go within and face that part of yourself in pain or distress. Maybe in finding that other space away from the chores of home and work you give yourself time to heal and grow. This is fine of course, just remember that when all is said and done you cannot run away from yourself.

Dear World

30th July

Let us talk today about the plight of mankind, his hopes, fears and misdemeanours. The light of consciousness shines upon the land and all its peoples. So, the reality of that relationship becomes seen. That is the good, bad and indifferent parts that make up the whole. We are none of us perfect and that is not the expectation, but it is expected of conscious and aware beings to modify their behaviour and practices when harmful ones are made apparent. We see these changes happening and that is good for all, even those slow to learn, for they may follow.

Dear World

31st July

There is a land that exists beyond the seas, forever just out of reach, except in our dreams. This Isle of the Blessed, this Holy Island holds all that you seek, yet cannot quite grasp. An Isle of plenty and rest for the soul. If you are worthy and with luck, you may be guided there on your inner journeying to rest, heal and rejuvenate before it is time to return from whence you came. The waters between hold clues to its nature and guardianship. To learn the secrets of the tides and waters is a lifetime's work, but worth the wait and effort.

Dear World

1st August

There is never so much that can be learned from a situation as that which is around you now. You have witnessed the best and worst of things. The time for waiting is over. Being reserved and shy is all very well, but necessity is the mother of invention and necessity decrees that now is a time to be more assertive and direct. This does not mean being reckless or inconsiderate, but taking considered action or decisions in good time. The world is still turning. Much water has passed under the bridge. Take heed of who is around you and listen to their stories. The weaving together of these stories brings understanding of the plight and direction in which you are all moving. Remember how it feels.

Dear World

2nd August

There is much to be said for ritualistic practice and celebration when performed in the correct spirit. It is engrained in the fabric of humanity to periodically mark and celebrate points of time, seasons and other milestones. The intersection between mankind and nature is vibrant at these times and the spirit of nature and humanity is raised by these activities. The bond is strengthened by these celebrations and memories imprinted onto the ether.

Dear World

3rd August

There is a time and season for all beings. The passage of time pauses only for the awakening of another epoch. You are all gathered inwardly wondering what is about to occur. You feel the fire of your spirit and the sharpening of the senses. You can hear the rhythm of your own breathing, as anticipation rises. So, what is to follow? What have you all been waiting for? Why are you gathered here and now? This is yet to be written, for you are all conspiring in its creation. It is enough to be ready and of generous spirit. Listen well and heed the call.

Dear World

4th August

So, the fire has burnt itself out for now and you feel a bit weary. That is ok, you cannot run around all the time, having too many irons in the fire. There is still heat in the embers. Rest a while. Take stock of where you are and what has befallen. The glowing embers can warm you and be more productive than a raging fire anyway. Look into the glow among the ashes and feel the warmth within.

Dear World

5th August

Despite the heat of the sun there is still sometimes a coldness within. Sometimes it is needed to balance the outer heat, helping you keep your cool among the hot-headed ones. Whether it is a gift from within, or an externally generated energy, it serves a purpose, but let it not extinguish the inner fire completely. Cool and calm is a virtue, cold and unfeeling is not. Let the ice maiden do her work and all will be well.

Dear World

6th August

So, the deed is done. Time to move on, let bygones be bygones. The path to enlightment necessitates occasional interruptions and annoyances. It is the way you deal with them, that changes as time moves on. Now you do not allow yourself to be swallowed up by the temporary emotion of a situation. Of course, you are affected and stirred by it, but you are learning to keep some perspective and distance. This allows yourself to observe and be more prudent in action and thought. The flow of life entails meetings with obstacles, some of which turn out to be fortuitous, others not. Do not take everything too personally. All is as it is meant to be.

Dear World

7th August

So, time has passed. The memory of forgotten childhood summers are in the splashes and screams of today's children. The heat of the day melts the rigid body and pauses the overactive mind. A distant memory of the summerlands brings comfort to the soul. Remembering happens not all at once, but in the piecing together of fragments of experiences and meetings with place that remind a soul of its wholeness. This is not something that can be learnt, it is an intuitive process that consciousness, when ready, will realise.

Dear World

8th August

There is much between heaven and earth unseen and that has always been so. Many are so involved in day-to-day life that they notice little in this regard. There are those among you who notice much more or have messages and insights to share. This path is not for all, but the awakening of some perception in this regard is desirable in most of humanity as time moves on. There are always moments of clarity and at other times the fog of unknowing, but patience and persistence in these matters is productive both in personal development and in the teaching and sharing of it.

Dear World

9th August

So, the work has begun. The interweaving of ideas and thoughts to create a new tomorrow have been incubating in the quiet months and in the re-emerging they will begin to encounter meetings with receptive, creative minds. Nothing is wasted, not time or resources. Ultimately everything is the compost of new growth and life returning. The restless wandering spirit and the spirit of home are jostling for ascendency, but each will have their time and fulfilment. Listen carefully to the inner calling and heed its call.

Dear World

10th August

So, there are many faces around you; some familiar, others not. Who is to know who will become familiar and who will not? Even those closest to you were strangers once. Do not erect barriers to friendship and new encounters. Like attracts like and as many of you have re-discovered aspects of yourselves during these unusual times, others may find themselves in harmony with these new characteristics and interests. Life needs life, love needs love.

Dear World

11th August

The art of life is in knowing its depths and subtleties. Pausing and reviewing the terrain can avoid much wasted energy and frustration. We are here to serve each other, not to be a slave or master. Each have their own mirrors that reflect life back at them. You may not see the world exactly as another, but just being aware that other perspectives are possible stands you in good stead. Sands shift and so do feelings. What is true today may not be true tomorrow. Feeling is believing.

Dear World

12th August

So, have you forgotten how to love, or discern what is and is not love? When you have been hurt in whatever way at the heart level, it becomes difficult to open-up again. We always encourage, to begin with, learning to love the beauty in nature, in all of creation. Move on to love all acts of random human kindness and then to love yourself. None of this is easy for those still in pain, but each step makes it a little easier. We are none of us immune to the knocks and scars of life, but showing a little love and kindness where you can opens a gateway to a better world for all.

Dear World

13th August

Let us try to understand the situation right now in the world. Much has been shaken up by this crisis and brought to the surface. Mismanagements, incompetence and corruption are finding it hard to hide, but heroism, kindness and love are finding more opportunities for expression. Unfortunately fear and suspicion sometimes stand in the way of altruism and also in the receiving of help. The breaking down of these barriers will help in the way forward.

Dear World

14th August

There is always something unforeseen waiting to surprise us. The children of the world run and play in war torn cities and pristine parks and forests alike. Their games reflect their experiences, but their imaginations see beyond their immediate environment and encounter an unlimited magical world of possibilities. Do not lose this hope with age and weariness of life. Let its wonder unfold before you, for it can and the multi-layered reality of life can be revealed. You are all children of spirit and earth, exploring the world around you. All things in this world uncovered are there for the taking and sharing.

Dear World

15th August

Night follows day as day follows night. There are those who deny the existence of darkness, or refuse to face it. There is a beauty in the healing depths of the unknown, or the light of possibility that arises from it. The modern mind needs the sanctity of the night temple to soothe the nervous tension of the day. The spiritual darkness filters the conscious thoughts down to what is most relevant and worthy of attention. This is also the work of the meditative and dream state. In this is the universal truth that in the darkness shines the star of truth and light.

Dear World

16th August

So, time moves on. Light changes its hue with the influence of seasons and mood. Your spiritual light is also influenced by the seasons of your life and your own mood. Consider light beyond light, beyond light, beyond light and love beyond love, beyond love, beyond love. These continuing waves and vibrations support and re-enforce each other, each one more subtle and finer than the one before. This is the nature of life in all its forms, here and beyond.

Dear World

17th August

Not all days are the same. The rules, routines and patterns of life are sometimes torn up, if even for just a day or so. Sometimes these moments shock you into necessary changes, or make you appreciate more the blessings of the life you have. Do not ponder too deeply on the consequences, but find your feet and live as you would seem fit and proper. Smile and remember the blessings which are around you.

Dear World

18th August

Life becomes you. Everything you experience in life shapes your personality and ultimately your soul. Like the work of a sculpture gradually taking form, this process goes on. Some of life's events you feel sharply like the imprint of the chisel, others work more slowly like the river that gradually cuts through rock, leaving a canyon in its wake. Is it art, craft or science that shapes your form? Or is it the mystical direction of a creative unseen power? However you see the process, you are walking on the path, being shaped along the way.

Dear World

19th August

It is never too late for reconciliation and forgiveness. Where misunderstanding meets misunderstanding, conflict may arise, or hurt, pain and loss. It is not for us to dictate your beliefs and manners, but we do guide your path towards the light that is the understanding of yourself and others. It is in your own interests to take the time and effort to try and perceive all angles and directions in viewing life on earth. It is easier to rest in the comfort of your own convictions, but the true spiritual and earth pioneer will walk the path less travelled to better understand what maketh man and what engenders compassion for all beings.

Dear World

20th August

Healing takes many forms, but it begins with trying to understand what it is that needs to be healed. Many wounds are invisible to the eye, they lie deep within. With experience you can observe the outer effects of inner wounds in behaviour and mannerisms, or eventually those emotional hurts may become manifest in the physical. It is not our responsibility to heal every malady, but to listen and bear witness to another's pain is often the first step towards their healing. If you cannot be close to the suffering one, hold them in the healing light from a distance and let the healing manifest through the spiritual realms to the spirit and whole being of the one in pain. In this we can all play our part.

Dear World

21st August

The world is your oyster, so they say. In many respects this is true. There are those who have travelled half-way around the world on a very small budget. Current circumstances would advise against that, but none of you are as limited as you may believe. The self-imposed limits to your horizons may be set by your own expectations, those of your peers, your ancestral inclinations or the tendencies of the society in which you find yourself. Responsibility is obviously a factor, but you also have a responsibility to be honest to yourself. The wind blows one way then another, but when it fills your sail see where it takes you.

Dear World

22nd August

Several years have passed since the becoming, the impulse to open the group soul of humanity. Windows were opened to your sacred earth that allowed the pouring forth of a certain energy into her depths. This has been slowly releasing into the fabric of the planet and those upon it. This is in order to awaken a new dawn for you all. Yes, a difficult interaction, but a re-organisation of principles of communication and means of engendering spiritual connection and manifestation. This has not been an easy process for any involved, but many are at one with the revealing. Feel the change within and around and accept it for what it is. You are not alienated from this energy. It is becoming you, finding alignment with your being and all earthly beings. This we give unto you.

Dear World

23rd August

Sit with us a while under the trees in fellowship. Listen to the birdsong and gentle rustling of the leaves. Hold hands in companionship and breathe the clear air of the forest. The fire glows brightly in the still of the early evening. Although there is silence, each knows how the other is feeling. The presence of all brings all there into peace, balance and harmony. In this simple act much is achieved. Peace to you all.

Dear World

24th August

Seven years is an age of man. Each life is divided into these segments. Each marks a turning point in the development of a soul living in this lifetime. If you look at a life you will see how these ages mark shifts in the personality as it matures and tries to adjust to the life around itself. There is a magic in the number that gives a fullness of experience, but just short of the completeness of an eight. Observe how this has been so in yourself and others.

Dear World

25th August

There is time and space enough for all of your ways. The idiosyncrasies of your individual path and life are gifted space to manifest. This needs to be true of all paths, given that they harm no other. The world is wide and deep and is home to a multitude of souls. There is no reason, save the fear and suspicion of others, that they cannot all find their place and means of spiritual connection and expression. Respect and consideration for self and others is a basic tenet of a harmonious life. Let this be so and the world will be a more peaceful one.

Dear World

26th August

The joy and stillness of the wood is a wondrous thing. It awakens the spirit within, the magical joyous child. The spirit of play and personal, ancestral memories awaken as you run and explore the world around. The world within awakens in harmony with this youthful enthusiasm; a strange but natural mix of enthusiasm, allowed by the peace and enclosure of the forest. Blessed are the children of the forest, for they always know when to run and hide, or help lost souls find their way.

Dear World

27th August

The ways and means to spirit are many and varied. It is not for all to fall to their knees and pray, but this takes nothing away from those that do. The world of nature has gateways that open perception to other worlds and nature itself teaches us about life and also spirit. A message may come in the sign of an animal, bird or encounter with a friendly tree. Others use the gateway of word, book and mind to hear the voice of spirit and open up the heart. Be it all of these or other means to feel more connected; it is the intent and consistency that pulls you through. All is as it should be.

Dear World

28th August

Synchronicity and opportunity go hand in hand. Despite the toiling of your individual will, life and progress can often be frustrating and even confusing at times. Accepting when divine forces are at work, either in a protective manner, or in guiding you along your path, is the wiser way to be. At those times you open yourself to the possibility of chance encounters and opportunities that flow more readily it seems and with less apparent effort. There is of course a time for will and determination, but knowing when to save your energy and trust in the flow of life and spirit is a valuable lesson learnt and a blessing received.

Dear World

29th August

So, we sit on a precipice looking into the valley below and what do you see? Is there movement or stillness? Does the river flow or is it dried up and the land parched and dry? Is it a land of plenty, or of lack? What moves towards you and who or what moves away? How does the scene make you feel? Is it constant or changing? Do you feel ready to fly across these lands? Does it feel like home or some long forgotten dream? Who is beside you at this vantage point? Seen or unseen, greet them, give thanks and remember that you can return.

Dear World

30th August

A soul floats through life looking for the light of recognition in another soul. For most this is an unconscious process, but when there is recognition it may come into conscious awareness. This may be true of place and person; the déjà vu of a place already known and the soul connection of a stranger unveiled. If you allow your awareness to recognise it, the soul lights twinkle like stars in the night sky, inexorably drawing you to those you need at this time in your life; an unchained process, unfettered by age, personality or gender. Be aware of your own light, for you may be a beacon to another soul. We are each other's guiding light.

Dear World

31st August

So, in the beginning there were many possibilities awaiting to unfold, but not all could become apparent at that time. Those other possibilities and frames of evolution are still in existence and are ready to take the place of this one if it falters on its evolutionary track. The impulse reverberating in the planet can change if stagnation is realised. There are strong spiritual forces behind these other chains of existence that are shifting in position and ready for their opportunity. It is not without reason that we explain this to you at this time. There is a tiring and weariness behind this evolution and it requires the individual and combined will of humanity and conscious existence to work with it, or accept the real possibility of dynamic and extreme change in this trajectory.

Dear World

1st September

So, the year turns and autumn approaches. Feelings of industriousness are interspersed with anxiety. The reach towards some routine and normality is made. Schools return in expectation of nations and parents. Rush hours appear again, a reminder of the point of stress. All will unfold and settle in its own time. It is not a time for regret and looking back, but to step forward with hope and trust.

Dear World

2nd September

They say seeing is believing, but is this necessarily true? It might be better to say feeling is believing, because most of you trust your feelings regarding even that which you cannot see. Life requires all to make judgments and decisions on that with which you might not yet be familiar. You use reason, maybe the advice of others, but also that which you may regard as a kind of sixth sense, in order to decide. This we know may not always be apparent to you, but you are using your spiritual faculties when you do this, it is just that because you have been doing this since you were very young that you have become unaware of what you do. This intuitive sensing of that which affects you and your environment is a gift open to all and a gateway to develop more subtle sensitivities for those that are willing and able.

Dear World

3rd September

Somewhere on the periphery of your consciousness you know there is a wealth of insight and wonders available to you. It is often just out of reach, but you do not know why. There is much to behold, but your modern world, distractions and noise disturb the ability to fine tune to the vibration needed in order to perceive clearly. We know you seek the peace and space needed to do this and are with you in this endeavour.

Dear World

4th September

So, when all is said and done there is much to be said for a quiet life, but quiet on the outside does not always mean quiet on the inside. Sometimes the mind fills the void left by social isolation. This can be beneficial if it allows contemplation and musing over relevant considerations. There is however always the habit of mind chatter, over stresses and worries that cannot settle. Part of the art of meditation is in allowing them their time and space, then letting them go.

Dear World

5th September

The landscape tells many tales, not least those told by the marks left by the passage of many travellers. From those passing through, to those whose names from long ago still hold their presence on mound, on farm, on field and wood. How long ago did they live upon the land? Their memories are rooted within it. It is hard to imagine many from our present times leaving their name upon the land, excepting a precious few. Walking the land or reading a revealing map awakens the potential tale of many a ghost or spirit still inhabiting it.

Dear World

6th September

The wind blows from one direction, then on another day from another. This is the way of life. When the wind blows from the west there is no point looking to the east for what may come towards you. This is a metaphor for life. It is prudent to go with the direction and flow that is currently prevailing. This is not to say ignore the existence of the others, for they will have their day and then when the wind is still, allow it into yourself. Let the peace prevail.

Dear World

7th September

Turning over a new leaf is an expression, but also an act of resolve. Turning a new page in the story of your life is a positive undertaking. There is a freshness that comes with starting a new book or writing in the first page of a new diary. What new adventures are about to begin? What new chapter is about to be written? All will be revealed a page at a time.

Dear World

8th September

Little ones have to learn so many skills when yet so young, to build a basis of survival for life. They need to learn how to stand up for themselves and also be able to interact with others. They are trying to understand how the world around them functions and what is or is not fair. So many names, so many numbers and how to be on time. To dress and undress when required and eat mostly in a healthy way. They learn through play of course and observation to, but no wonder sometimes they run a little wild. Let them imagine worlds of play, which later bring solutions, as adults free their weary minds and play with ideas instead of childhood toys.

Dear World

9th September

Tiredness of mind and body are to be expected at times in this changing, uncertain world. Awakening to new perceptions requires adjustment of body and mind, as they are not in isolation from each other. Connectivity in body sometimes reflects connection with the outer world. Joints are the gateways between energetic impulse and movement. The flow of impulse to movement in life is sometimes restricted by both personal and outer factors and our relationship towards them. Too much or too little of that activity, can affect the connectivity important to healthy body and mind.

Dear World

10th September

You wait and listen to the tick-tock of time passing, waiting for it all to pass and then what. A hundred plans and dreams made, then abandoned. A lover won and then lost. What are you really waiting for? Is it with you already, that which you seek, or are you clutching at straws? The tick-tock of time continues. The sun rises and sets and the year turns. You are here now, that is what matters.

Dear World

11th September

So, you stand at a crossroads not knowing which way to turn. There is a window of opportunity now to make a difference. You can all walk the path of least damage to the world and others. It is your choice to make and to follow. We can light the way and try to lighten your burden, but the steps are yours to make. You cannot always see what lies over the horizon it is true, but let your inner light and heart guide you in this matter.

Dear World

12th September

It is strange how different days have different feels. Some days wrap themselves around you in a nurturing way. At these times you know you are supported and cared for, even if you know not where from. These days teach you that it is ok to self-nurture and be kind to yourself. Allow a little rest and relaxation. The busy, striving days will return soon enough. So, take these moments and remember that none of this time is wasted.

Dear World

13th September

Let us pray. Hold hands together in spirit. This can still be done, though few can get together in person. When you close your eyes and reach out to those, like yourself, who may be tired of the fear, restriction and anxiety caused by this ongoing disease, they may join you in spirit. Others join hands with them until you have a circle that surrounds nations and the whole world. When you feel this connection and intent, join in your own way in heartfelt prayer for healing to all and the fading of the stress, illness and circumstances that caused it. Visualise a caring, sustainable, loving world for all beings and feel that reality through hand and heart. Continue to hold this vision until it fades. Return to your own space and time and give thanks for blessings received and given.

Dear World

14th September

Water can have a magnetic pull on the human spirit. The draw of a stream or shoreline on a hot summer's day promises something; an equalization of water within, a cooling and elemental realisation. The waters also offer us reflection, sometimes in a literal sense, but always in an emotional way. Being close to flowing or tidal water reminds us of our changing moods and the natural cycles that lie behind them. Still waters give us pause to feel what is real inside and allow a moment to reflect. Stormy waters on a dark brooding day can also draw and reflect another side of life and our own changing elemental nature. Water within meets water without; this is the blessing.

Dear World

15th September

Talking is good for body and soul. That is in expressing your thoughts and feelings to others. Self-reflection is important and healthy, but to voice your intent brings a release that your body appreciates. There is a time for silence and a time to be heard. Remember your voice is a gift to be used wisely, but shared freely.

Dear World

16th September

So, time for a re-think maybe. What has gone before is a precursor to what is likely to follow, but alternatives are always available to the determined and strong of heart. A truth as yet unspoken is waiting to be revealed. Hidden depths are apparent in all beings, but shy to be revealed. What is to be in this unfolding story before you? Only time will tell, but time often holds onto secrets until an opportune moment.

Dear World

17th September

Sometimes, even from a state of deep tiredness, you can reach a feeling of bliss. If you are still for long enough and allow the healing that is waiting for you to do its work, this feeling may arise. When the mind finally settles and the body begins to heal, an almost euphoric sensation can slowly rise up the body and lift up your heart. This is a state of grace for which you are deserving, but always most thankful.

Dear World

18th September

There seems such a fragility to your current stability and happiness. The changing world around you creates fluctuations in your emotions that can cause feelings of anxiety or sometimes depression; as hopes are raised and then dashed, almost in the same breath. The only consolation is that this pattern is becoming familiar and you are learning to look within for courage and strength, which you had forgotten was there. Take companionship when you can and be your own best friend. The rest is as yet undiscovered.

Dear World

19th September

There is something close to your heart that is causing you pain. It may be loss, or love unopened. Also, the hurt of feeling misunderstood can find its way to rest by the heart. The joy of love waiting to open and express itself can feel not unlike the sadness of love lost, when it is in a state of tension. This is why we urge you to look towards love for all beings, for in that there is always capacity to give and receive. All things must pass. Remember this.

Dear World

20th September

Many years have passed since the beginning of this passage of time. There are matters yet to be resolved that exist from earlier epochs and have not yet evolved out of them. By this we mean that an evolutionary process is completing now that needs to resolve itself before the new paradigm can begin to awaken in you all. This is why many of you feel not quite one way or the other. It is as if you are between different time and space realities. This will resolve itself in good time. Your awareness means that you are already half-way there.

Dear World

21st September

To whom it may concern. There is a need to be more considerate to each other at these times. No one is in this alone. The action of one impacts on all. This is true of most aspects of life, not just the current situation. The 'I'm alright Jack' attitude is no longer really appropriate. Consideration of the impact of one's actions on the whole of humanity and the environment are all too apparent. This epidemic has taught this at least. Yes, be individual in spirit, but universal in outlook. This is the only way to move forward.

Dear World

22nd September

So, life begins as summer ends. This might seem a contradiction, but the darker, longer nights and cooler days lend themselves to more reflection and consolidation of ideas. In this is included more learning and considered action. In the autumn we plough fields and dig gardens. Although this seems a bedding down for the winter, it starts a process of metabolism in the soil that is echoed in the fabric of our own lives.

Dear World

23rd September

Lives matter. No life is lived in vain. Whether your life is long and filled with notable achievements, or short and limited by disease, poverty or disability, it still has an impact on the group soul of humanity and the planet. The lives of others effect each of you, whether that is an unrelated life, but one that touches your emotions or inspires you; or someone close whose day-to-day life shaped your personality and view of the world. Lives of animals and plants also influence through the shaping of environment and in the individual comfort, presence and beauty which they can bring, but also in their own inter-related existence, irrespective of human interaction. Even the life of someone that highlights the wrongs of how to live a life has a teaching value that makes others strive to do better. Also, in valuing your own gift of life you open the way to appreciate the lives of others.

Dear World

24th September

There are forever truths and temporary truths. That is that there are universal truths that are always apparent, whatever time or place you are living in; the law of karma for example. These truths follow us from lifetime to lifetime and therefore are familiar to our soul and in alignment with it. When our soul encounters actions that are not adhering to these truths, it knows that something is not quite right, if only at a subconscious level. Temporary truths are those that can be proved or illustrated in a certain period of time or space. This is because certain conditions exist in order to stimulate certain developments of evolution and these truths govern these pockets of existence. They do not override universal truths or exist beyond them, but in dynamic periods of change such as this, they will be apparent.

Dear World

25th September

There is something that needs to be said about the change of seasons. As it happens in the northern hemisphere at this time of year, we turn from summer to autumn; from the time of heat, sun and ripening, to the time of harvest home, consolidation and drawing in. The countryside bears witness to many circles of stones and ancient monuments that marked these changing seasons, because they were important to the agricultural life of community, but also to their psychic and spiritual life. These times were points of recognition, celebration and thanksgiving that still resonate within us now, if we take a little time to feel and listen. The heartbeat of earth and sky that is a constant, grounds us to the ancestral and personal memories of seasons gone and seasons yet to come.

Dear World

26th September

So, the time has come to face the situation that you are all facing. It is often said that there is more than one way to crack a nut. This is certainly true in working towards an end to this pandemic situation. The path of control is one way certainly, that is in controlling movement and exposure. Another is the path of cure and prevention. Although this can take time to perfect, it has worked before. We know some are opposed to this medical intervention, but all solutions are god led in the end. The other path is one of resolution. By this we mean overcoming through resilience and fortitude, after all in the end this is what gets you through most struggles, individually and collectively. We watch with interest the rise and fall of humanity's outlook. The light falls one way, then another as former practices and behaviours are exposed as no longer acceptable in these new days. The shadow resists, but ultimately life is the winner.

Dear World

27th September

The longing in you seeks fulfilment, but sometimes you know not what you seek. The passing of time makes you weary of the task and fearful of ever reaching the end. It is always the journey that matters of course, but that may be little comfort when heart and soul yearn for something just out of reach. When distractions fall by the wayside, the nakedness of your quest feels all too apparent. It is ok to feel a little lost now and then. Tomorrow the journey starts anew.

Dear World

28th September

There is a sweetness in the air on a fine autumnal day; the scent of fresh turned earth, ripened fruit and air still warm, but tinted with the crispness of colder days approaching. On days like these we give thanks for our harvest, in whatever form that takes and take a breath of that expectant air. Even in this year of all years you may be surprised what harvest you have gained. You may feel the aching body that bears witness to the effort, but remember to give thanks to the unseen forces that have helped you bring it in.

Dear World

29th September

Hello my dear friends. So, what is it that ails you? Is it the stress and strain of life, or doors as yet unopened? One day is much like another on the surface, but can feel very different within. We all carry burdens, seen and unseen, so do not be unkind to yourself and others in judgment. Take help when offered, but do not expect it. Give of yourself freely when able, but do not enslave yourself to others. Peace is your birth-right and will come.

Dear World

30th September

Seven years from now there will be many changes in your world. These are to be for the better it is hoped. Many bridges are still to be crossed until then of course. It is hard for many of you to perceive a positive view of the future currently, we understand this, but step by step much can be achieved. Nobody is being asked to abandon all that they hold dear, but to consider that which others hold dear. This is not such a difficult undertaking, it just requires a little determination and perseverance in order to manifest. We trust you all in this.

Dear World

1ˢᵗ October

Days go by; years go by and for what purpose? The passage of time appears linear, but behaves in a circular fashion. Lives fall into repeating patterns by which we measure progress, if any, on our path in life. You may spend a lifetime contemplating the meaning of life, or not consider it at all. Some are content to accept life in a two-dimensional aspect; you're born, you live and you die view of the world. This is not untrue, but as these teachings will have reminded you, there are many aspects to life and reasons to bless every year and day that passes.

Dear World

2nd October

Life is what you make it, so they say and what do you make of your life. Most will have mixed feelings. At times it is accepted that you may have a certain level of satisfaction with your lot in life. At other times you may feel dissatisfied and unfulfilled. Sometimes we are our own harshest critic and susceptible to seeking perfection in our endeavours, or near to it. Although it is always good to strive to do the best that you can, it is humbling to remember that there will always be other factors that may impact on your aims, be that in a positive or negative manner. It is just how things are. A maturing outlook, honed through experience, will usually realise the right level of expectation and therefore pleasure to be gained from that which is accomplished for self or others.

Dear World

3rd October

Having time is a blessing bestowed upon you. All the times you have not had time come to mind and yet you know not what to do with it. The pause caused by the virus situation allowed a slowing down of life for many and the luxury of doing a lot or doing little. We are still in uncertain times and taking time to pause and breathe is not time wasted. There will be time enough for moving and doing with intent. Somewhere on the edge of time lay possibilities unfolding. Be kind to yourself and allow life to be.

Dear World

4th October

The effort required to make positive change in the world is proportionate to the number involved in the undertaking. This is true whether it be small behavioural changes, signing petitions, planting trees or praying for world peace and healing. The effect multiplies exponentially with the number involved. Having said this, someone has to be the first, so do not be put off from your efforts in this respect if at first you feel that you are fighting a lone battle. There will be others unknown to you following the same inspiration to initiate that change for the better. So, whether your efforts appear subtle or dynamic, continue with good heart. That is all that matters.

Dear World

5th October

Every day has its own existence. That is that it has its own story to tell that can happen independently of any other day. In this way think of each day as a possibility that although obviously influenced by other days, is not bound by them. By this attitude it helps in taking a day at a time and to some extent be born again into each one. As we enter the dark half of the year, this attitude may help avoid succumbing to a pattern of thinking that loses hope and self-belief. We are all shaped by the times and circumstances around us, but we need not be defined by them.

Dear World

6th October

We are here for such a short time in the big scheme of things. Mankind's journey into earthly existence is a manyfold one, but not without precedent. Life has existed before the advent of humankind and will continue beyond his era. It is true that on an energy and spirit level nothing truly dies, but when viewing from a point in space, which is what gives spirit the feeling of existence, time turns and passes. The evolution of humanity is at a crux, but not because of its own achievements, more so its relationship to other existences. As it has been shown, there is much to be learnt in this matter.

Dear World

7th October

Sitting pretty is a phrase used to describe someone who is content with their current lot and is happy to sit put and look after it. It can also refer to a potentiality that exists from that position. There are many in this current situation sitting pretty. They may even be benefitting from it. There is not necessarily an immorality in this, but there may be a stagnation if they are not considering their motivation and position. In a crisis there is a seeking of security by everyone and that is a natural process, but to what degree one person's security is another's imprisonment or poverty is the question that needs to be heard. That is all.

Dear World

8th October

There seems to be a point of balance between passivity and action where healing takes place. Too much of either can prevent or at least delay its progress. Periods of passivity can help restore energy, allow contemplation on next moves and the opening of receptive faculties. Too much passivity can lead to apathy, weakness or depression. In contrast too much activity can cause tension, exhaustion and stress. The right amount of activity though is stimulating, engenders strength and health, leading to a good mental balance. We know it is difficult to move from one extreme while there, but awareness is the first step. This is not just important for the individual, but also for the whole.

Dear World

9th October

There is a question being asked of you which is: do I have the means and power to do anything against this pandemic? The other question is: is now the time or is it still futile? It is true that everything happens for a reason; so many lessons are being learnt through the impact of and reaction to the virus. Things have moved on though and we believe that it may soon be time to do the spiritual work required to assist in this process. No more doubts in this respect. You can all see that this disease is but a sign of the bigger crisis effecting earth. Everybody has their personal responsibility in this regard, but you must work to your own strengths to enable change and healing. In this we are always with you.

Dear World

10th October

Days go by, weeks and years go by, millennia pass all in the blink of an eye. It is all a matter of perspective. To you a day can sometimes seem like an eternity, but as time is relative to space, if you shrink space, time follows suit. You all want to extend your lives, so do not want to contemplate the short duration of a human age. However, in order to consider evolution on the earth plane, it becomes necessary to move yourself to this perspective. A grandparent may observe a year in the life of a grandchild and recall how long every year seemed at that age, compared to a year in their life now. As you all pass through stages of life, so does the planet. It may help to view your current situation on earth like an adolescent emerging into adulthood. It does not happen smoothly, or without some upset on the way, but it falls on parents and carers to guide with love during this process. In this task we are all blessed.

Dear World

11th October

Dearest one, we are not without compassion when we look at your predicament. There are ways in which we can help and in others we cannot. The living of life is for you all to partake in, with all its highs and lows. This is the passage of the soul. We can guide you towards one way or another and at these times higher spirits are guiding us to make you live simpler lives, at least for a while. This is important not only to protect yourselves and planet, but to allow absorption and integration of new energy. For some this has already happened, so do not be frustrated, just be a springboard for others to follow if this is you. Feel the possibility of what is arising.

Dear World

12th October

We watch over all that matters in your world, from trees and bees, to mountains and knees, all are within our realm of influence. We are spirits of nature and all that is living or has been living is in our care. We aim to bring all into balance and natural harmony; from the smallest flower to forests and continents. You do well to remember that humankind are part of nature, not separate from it and those who deny this deny their own true existence. We are troubled in our work at these times, though we know most of you work with us. Feel the rhythms and flows of nature's call and all will be well with us and you.

Dear World

13th October

Sometimes when you are called upon to do healing work you can feel the energy spiralling through your body and in the palms of your hands. This means that there is healing work to be done. If there are none around who seek your aid you can heal yourself or send healing to those in need. Using this energy encourages its flow. Remember there are always situations, places and mother earth that needs our healing too.

Dear World

14th October

Is there anything that would make your life better at this time? You worry about yourself and others in these turbulent times we know. So, in taking a moment to take a little care of yourself and allow some joy, you become less of a worry to yourself and those around you. It is not always possible, but allowing a simple pleasure if it does no harm, is an action that lightens the load for yourself and others and also encourages them to follow suit.

Dear World

15th October

It is often said by us that fortune favours the brave. This may be true, but bravery takes many forms. Yes, there are the outward signs of bravery, those who stand up for themselves or other people and causes. There is also the hidden bravery of those who keep on with their mission in life despite physical, emotional and mental pain or financial hardship. Anyone who faces a fear is brave in that undertaking. We are not without sympathy for these plights and know that fortune may not always appear in the most obvious form, but it is there if you care to see it.

Dear World

16th October

There is still much to be said about that which is as yet undiscovered. Between heaven and earth lies much unseen, but which yet is impacting on your world. Do not forsake the visionaries, for they see more than most. It is not for the blinkered ones to decide what is truth, for how will they know.

Dear World

17th October

Woodland spirits welcome the seeking human spirit. As senses open to touch, smell and sounds that remind the body what is real, the chattering mind falls silent. There is life even in the decay, death feeds life. The primal, sentient you does not fall from spirit, but merge with it, as spirits are lifted by this encounter.

Dear World

18th October

The worst lies are the ones that we tell ourselves. These are often about our own motivations, which are usually multiple in nature. Although you may have higher ideals that initiate your actions, the very human needs for security, companionship and acknowledgement also come into play. This is especially true when the motivation and energy to continue starts to dim, as the impression of loss or self-sacrifice rises into consciousness. We are none of us perfect and must answer first to ourselves. Ask yourself if you would wish your predicament on others, without the understanding of the motivation for honest human needs.

Dear World

19th October

Life becomes you. You are shaped by the events and influences that happen during your lifetimes. Yes, you all arrive with certain characteristics and dispositions; the birthing of soul into body allows this, but the reason you are born into earthly lives is to experience, grow and evolve. In doing this you not only develop your soul, but bring something to the group soul of humanity, heal ancestral lines and help life and the evolving earth around you.

Dear World

20th October

Smile and the world smiles with you, it is said and it is not without merit. Even the physical act of smiling reminds you of the pleasure behind it. A smile is an infectious thing and an infection that we do not wish to curb. It costs nothing, but if it brightens someone's day then it is priceless. Do not compare your life to others or be oppressed by life's worries. Spreading a little happiness is well overdue in these difficult times. Begin as you mean to go on.

Dear World

21st October

Several years ago, there was an incident that foreshadowed what came to follow. It is not for us to give detail, but it is withheld only for karmic considerations. We are talking about an international level of influence. Enough said for now, what matters is the repercussions that were set apace, resulting in some of your current problems. So how is this to be addressed or remedied? You ask. In your spiritual ways you must seek the seed of light that overcomes; the light within the shadow that is already there. You have the power individually and collectively to focus on this to burn away that which is not relevant or in harmonious evolution. In this we are all entrusted.

Dear World

22nd October

It is not without some distinction and renown that the druid people have become known. To most they are synonymous with white robes and Stonehenge, but their true connection and power goes much deeper. To the ancient celtic peoples of this land, the connection to the land and its spirits was everything and still is. They undertook much sacrifice of self, in order to make this so. Like other ancestral beliefs, it is still very much alive and informing us today of the crisis which we are facing. They say to you at this time, 'Let us walk with you in the forest of belief and renown, where futures are seeded. Remember your ancestors at this time and feel the resonance of their spiritual love.'

Dear World

23rd October

The sacredness of life takes on many forms and some we are too blind to see; of branch, of feather and warm-blooded life we are all too familiar. There is also sacredness in rock and stone, as the ancients knew all too well. The sacredness of hill and mountain is plain for all to see, where sky and storm first meet earth and sun and moon hold sway. It is not for us to understand why earth and rock was made, but to hold its beauty in our heart and bless each dawning day.

Dear World

24th October

Spirits of the sacred wells and springs have hidden depths and meaning. They know to read your heart and feel the way you are feeling. Chosen human guardians watched over these sacred springs and when they passed over, their spirits maintained that connection. They remember their human bond and their watery one. They know their destiny and seek only the means to fulfil it and the recognition of their existence. Their service is to humanity, nature and the world, in this common aim you will find connection and healing.

Dear World

25th October

Sometimes the body needs to rest and so does the mind. The difficulty lies in finding a space of peace and relaxation in which to rest it. Calming the nerves of the need to do something, at least for a while, is a start. The feeling soul is constantly sending and receiving sensory input from near and far to better understand the world around it. These times have called for much sensing and adjustment we know, but you need to be healed also. Allow the space to recuperate and then your work can begin again.

Dear World

26th October

Encounters of the random kind are more infrequent in these times. The déjà vu of people or place that awakened something in our soul are more restricted as lives have become so. It is important to still be open to these possible interactions despite the physical masking, for they often reveal something about the journey of the self at that moment. These encounters at a particular time and space reveal a recognition of the inner reflected in the outer world.

Dear World

27th October

Never before in the history of humanity on this planet has there been so much happening simultaneously around the world. In times past there has been unique evolvements and shared ones, like pyramids being erected in different parts of the world. What you may see as political and social changes are resulting from a spiritual impulse feeding into the minds and spirit of your peoples. This is also simultaneously aligning with soul changes in the earth itself.

Dear World

28th October

There is a way in which we are like puppets in a puppet theatre with our strings being pulled. To the audience the puppet has a character, with strengths and weaknesses. The observer knows that the strings are being pulled by one above, but at times sides with the character hoping that its personality can guide the puppeteer. In some ways in life we are aware of that connection for better or worse and maybe ultimately the puppeteer wishes us to pull our own strings anyway.

Dear World

29th October

Love takes many forms, many of which are unnoticed by the potential recipient. The avenues of expression are many faceted and take the form most favoured and available to the sender. This also depends on their relative openness, shyness, or ability to communicate. At times, all that is asked for is a reaction or recognition of existence. In this way many seeds are sown or fall on fallow ground. Even if the sentiment is not reciprocated immediately, it is honourable to show kindness and a gentle encouragement to the sender. Remember that it is wise to graciously receive love if it is freely sent, from whatever source.

Dear World

30th October

Between earth and heaven, the spiritual plane, there is a bridge of crossing. At this time of year, the bridge is open for your loved ones to easier meet again with you in spiritual form. Hold them close in heart and mind and light a candle for them, to guide the way. Recall the gift of their lives and the path that led to yours. It is a simple yet profound truth that allows this lifting of the veil. Remember that you are being reminded of the gift of life, through awareness of the transition that is death.

Dear World

31ˢᵗ October

We are addressing you all now at this time of crisis on your earth, as worlds collide the debris is plain to see. Be united by what you share, not divided by what is different. As we said before the paradigm that is foremost is one of co-operation leading to solution in all spheres of evolution and existence. Spin the wheel of this new dynamic, not the declining one that is behind you. Blessed are the way-showers and constant ones. All is not lost, just faltering. Move on beyond the clouds of doubt and fear, for we are but a step behind you. Nothing you do now is without purpose.

Dear World

1st November

Days go by, one by one. Many have passed in your lifetime and others will follow. So, remember when you have difficult or painful days that they will pass. Each day is a moment of time revealing itself in space. Your awareness of it, is what allows its existence in your world. It is in your power to change or define your relationship to that day and therefore any day. Think about it and observe the result.

Dear World

2nd November

Dear friends, do not be saddened by your new restrictions. There is a balance to be struck in lifetimes as well as days and weeks. When you look back at your lives of busy-ness, how often have you had extended periods of reflection. The frustrations are all too plain to see, but as it has been said before, nothing is wasted, especially times of silence and rest. Focus and renewal will follow at the right moment. For now, be content with life as you find it.

Dear World

3rd November

The art of listening is not wasted on you. It is rarer than you think in all honesty. Many hear, but few really listen. Even psychically, when connecting to spiritual worlds, you are not just listening for words in your mind, but a feeling or thought impression that is giving expression through the medium of spoken or written word. Often the feeling is stronger than the words; almost at times too much for words, but the words come and that is all that is asked at this time.

Dear World

4th November

On the inner planes you can meet with many, from those who are living, those that have passed over and discarnate beings. The link is astral, emotional. The living beings may be known or unknown to you, but share something with your vibration at that time or wish to. The travelling soul gives and receives much information at these times, even if words are not obvious. We are talking about a calm and at least partially conscious encounter, as in journeying or meditation. This is not the chaotic confusion of the dream state, although at times of lucidity the dreamworld can also reach this level.

Dear World

5th November

It is not without difficulty that this situation has manifested. We can see shifts in consciousness that are beginning to manifest and allow openings of hope for more beneficial situations to arise. Reduce the fear within yourself and others. Take necessary precautions and then make plans.

Dear World

6th November

Something needs to be said about the nature of being. By this we mean the balance between thought, action and presence. Most of you are living in a reactionary way, responding to stimuli from all sources, regardless of their immediate relevance to yourself. Of course, to some extent all beings are affected by all, but it is desirable in these tumultuous times to adopt a presence that is calm in the storm. Be connected to earth and your spiritual self with all that feeds it. Understand that others have fears and concerns which cause them to react in certain ways. This is not always personal to you. By developing an aura of compassion and understanding, yet maintaining some degree of self-containment, you are more able to be of service to self and others.

Dear World

7th November

To stand on a moonlit shore and gaze out to sea as the moon reflects on the gentle waves, awakens many feelings and makes others slip away. The timeless romanticism and soulful pull of the scene reminds us of the close relationship between contentment and melancholy. There seems at times little more than a breath of wind or a single wave to separate these moods.

Dear World

8th November

Leaders come and leaders go, nations shrink and nations grow. The impetus behind the leadership continues. It is an energy of expression waiting to be heard through a vessel of power. The force itself is not good or bad, but it works sometimes as a catalyst, at others as a driving force to ultimately create a better world and that ultimate force for change is beneficial in nature. It is not all about the leadership, but a leader reflects aspects of the personality of the majority and helps them to become conscious of those aspects and decide whether to refine or discard them. It is another part of the cycle of evolution, there for all to see.

Dear World

9th November

It is not without some regret that pain has need to come upon some of you. It is not always understood that ultimately we are protecting the soul and its growth. At times, bodily restrictions are all that can prevent self-harm or destructive paths. Having said that, not all pain is a result of these measures. The young soul needs to learn to withstand some physical and emotional knocks and scars, as does any young person. Some of you carry the pain of others, because you would rather do that than see others suffer. You need to learn to let it go. Empathy is of the moment, not an invitation to carry another's burden. So, true relief from pain cannot be achieved without aligning one's soul with its best destiny. Healing in part endeavours, as much as is able, to remind body and soul of this truth.

Dear World

10th November

Memories are made and held, sometimes for a moment, sometimes for a lifetime. It is not for us to discern what is most precious. The emotional memory goes deeper than memory of pure fact. It is all very well remembering something because it is interesting or necessary for a job or exam, but anything that is connected to a strong emotion runs deep, sometimes beyond the present lifetime. In the sadness of memory illness that effects so many, it is the emotional memories that linger longest, this is why music is a great healer in this respect.

Dear World

11th November

It is to be expected that the mourning continues. There are generations alive that remember the two great wars, or the wars of their fathers and father's fathers. We know the plight of women and animals too. How long will this continue you ask? It is important to remember the suffering of war and the apparent futility, for it discourages too urgent a precipitation into another. That is a desirable aim. Each generation asks of the next if they are willing to stand up for what is collectively agreed to be right and also if they acknowledge the sacrifice of their ancestors.

You are living in a time of re-analysing of the past, both personal and collective. This is a necessary exercise, but it is prudent to remember that what has gone before has led to now. In the present there is much to be thankful for, as well as much to cause concern. If mistakes and abuses are to be condemned, then success and progress should be praised and deliverance blessed with remembrance of those who went before. Each generation has its challenges. Those who judge too harshly will be judged by the same measure.

Dear World

12th November

The events of the last year are a forerunner of that which is yet to come. By that we do not mean that all will be bad, but there will be change on all levels. The desire is for all to keep up, as this makes life smoother for all with less need for stagnation and hold ups to allow for the unenlightened ones to awaken. It is not without some trepidation that we all move forward, for that which is familiar feels more stable. There will come a time when the new world view has more stability than the old, so it is well to be aware of this and sit yourself among its roots. All is relevant and in proportion to the level of push needed. We salute you all for what has been achieved and wait in the wings to be called.

Dear World

13th November

We came, we saw, we conquered; so the Roman motto goes. However, it is not just the Romans who acted in this way. Whether it is the destruction of wildlife habitat for roads, rail or building, or the expansion of a nation's borders, the same arrogance applies. All nations have been guilty of this in the past and many still are. Beware also of corporate subjugation in this respect. Nations withdraw their responsibilities as huge companies cross borders with impunity in their quest for profit. It is time for the voice of those that care to be heard, for they are the majority. No longer can the world stand by while species are lost, indigenous peoples lose their land and huge divisions in wealth and opportunity prevail. Unity in consciousness and focus can move mountains. Soon there will be a tidal wave of energy waiting to be expressed positively in the world, as slowly restrictions eventually ease. Let it be harnessed wisely for the best intent.

Dear World

14th November

How is it that the world we see around us can seem so different from one day to another? What you see or perceive is a reflection of your inner beliefs and inner existence. Your inner sense is mutable to a large extent, effected by the moon, thoughts, memories, soul experience and current emotions. These in turn are affected by sensory input from your surroundings; interactions with others, being in nature and media influences. So outer world effects inner world which effects perception of the outer world. Sometimes the effect is rapid, at others it happens over a period of time, but there is an energetic exchange between these worlds; a spiralling in and spiralling out, as illustrated by the labyrinth. Meditating upon or walking a labyrinth can help increase awareness of this process and settle it into a balanced state of equilibrium.

Dear World

15th November

There is a beauty in chaos that is not always easy to appreciate. You think that you need order and stability to live, but a certain amount of chaos is needed to stir things up and create new pathways and solutions. Sometimes only out of chaos do we find out that the combination of A and X is the solution to our problem. It is true that no one can live in chaos for too long, but if we do not allow moments of it, it will come and find us anyway.

Dear World

16th November

It is said that there are three types of people in the world: the foolhardy, the wise and the desperate. At first this may seem too narrow a parameter in which to group humanity, but it certainly works in some measure. Of course, an individual may fluctuate between all three states at different times however they may regard themselves. All types have some value to offer. The fool may be disparaged for his lightness of mood and random behaviour, but this also allows him to break through conventional barriers and be privy to more than most. The wise man or woman provides balance, reason and ancient knowledge where it is needed, but can be subject to tension and rigidity because of constant self-checking. So, what of the desperate ones, surely they have little to offer but disruption? you say. Sometimes out of desperation comes the impetus for change, breaking through barriers and outdated practices. History shows that social evolution has often come from the catalyst of a few desperate ones. It is for you to decide if this model fits and where in it you currently lie.

Dear World

17th November

So, when your time has come and all is behind you, what is your future? The veil of spirit comes before you and lifts enough to see the path. When your time comes you will not be alone on your journey if you listen for the call. The pull of those you leave behind will hurt a while, but as spirit and heart lift to your new world, the binds begin to release. There is time to say your goodbyes spiritually if not physically. Follow the path of light and the family in spirit who greet you. Your experience will be shaped by your beliefs, but under the influence of powers beyond them.

Dear World

18th November

We listen, we heal, we teach and advise. That is the destiny and purpose of those who choose the path of spiritual service, whether that be from here in the spiritual dimension or the spiritual ones living on the earth plane. It is a multi-faceted and potentially rewarding undertaking in terms of satisfaction and the blessing of helping others. At times it seems futile and irrelevant in a material world, but these illusions are temporary. We are all playing the long game in this respect.

Dear World

19th November

It is not without some regret that we say to you that there are still more restrictions and difficulties to come. The road ahead is not smooth or straight and sometimes misty. Much effort has occurred in these recent times, so do not weaken now. New hope is just around the corner. Keep on keeping on. There is much to be said for taking a day at a time and it will stand you all in good stead in the long run. Nothing lasts forever and these shadow times will pass. Remember what is important and hold true to it when you all move beyond this impasse.

Dear World

20th November

Hello world. There is a reason for everything that is happening in your world right now, much as it is an inconvenience to many of you. The way of the world is filled with mysteries and none more so than the mystery of time and fortune. Many of you look at your current lives and do not know what to plan or where to direct your energies. So, you whirl around in a state of confusion or nervousness. We implore you to try and focus on the bigger picture and direct your mental energy on that. In knowing that many are feeling frustrated on their path in life, awaken compassion and kindness for everyone thus suffering. If we are to emerge better than we entered this year, then collective awareness and resolution are essential.

Dear World

21ˢᵗ November

In times long ago, before rock was rock and earth was earth, great spirits of the land arose, who had intent before they had form. Out of the chaos of creation their will shaped mountain, river and stream as it was then. Slowly these spirits sank into union with their aspects of creation and there they still abide. To modern man this reality has been lost through disconnection and disinterest. In these remembering times, as feet return to earth, it is in the interest of man and earth to reacquaint themselves with these primal enactors, for in this power we are all rooted. In understanding this earth birth, we awaken that same wisdom that comes from the understanding of our own birth. In this truth we are blessed indeed.

Dear World

22nd November

It is a surprise to some that we do not intervene in circumstances like these that you are all facing. We are working with individuals and organisations to try and bring things back into balance. Most things happen with incarnate human effort aided by divine inspiration and guidance. When you watch a child grow, you cannot do everything for them, or they will never learn how to achieve things for themselves and solve problems. You encourage and help them to develop. Spirit to human help works in this manner also. We are all helping each other grow and thrive.

Dear World

23rd November

There is little chance for self-aggrandisement in these times of separation. In performing to invisible or silent audiences there is little to inflate or pamper the ego. We are all learning that not every deed needs to be outwardly acknowledged, although on some level nothing goes unnoticed. We are all sowing seeds of a forest yet to grow. In that knowledge you can have satisfaction. One day your work and kindness will bear fruit. For now, it is enough that you look towards this future with hope.

Dear World

24th November

There is always a new song to be heard and an old one to be sung. The rhythm of life is matched by the soundtrack that surrounds it. An old song or tune can recount a hundred memories and a new one can help imprint many more. There is also something deeper in this. Everything and everybody has their own song waiting to be heard or felt. Give space to allow the performance of others, as in this manner your own song will be heard.

Dear World

25th November

There is an inward quickening at this time of year, a building excitement as we head towards the celebration of yule, Christmas and the winter solstice. There is an ancient contract, in the northern hemisphere at least, that celebrates the still small light and growing sun. There is no obligation to continue with all that has gone before, but where that is rooted in the relationship between the land and its people it lives within the DNA and demands recognition. Many cultures have different ways of expressing the festival of light of course and all have tradition and momentum. For now, it is enough to feel the vibration of the coming season within your own being and soul family. Prepare to celebrate in a way at one with the time and space in which we are present.

Dear World

26th November

There is always a solution to a problem, an answer to a riddle and a means to cross an obstacle in your path. You are all learning to react and then let go, as the stresses of a continuously changing outlook effect you all. This adaptability will stand you in good stead eventually and is doing so already. Life is for living, it has already been said, but there are many ways of living. It is ok to take a moment to look back at what you have managed to cope with. You are all stronger than you think. This does not mean that you are not without pain or suffering, but that you are finding ways to move beyond it.

Dear World

27th November

It is not without some resistance that this situation has occurred. The waves of emotions that wash over the world are confusing for some, debilitating for others. Sometimes there is a need to be still and separated from others while the change in you becomes real and manifest. It is a temporary measure to allow fulfilment of the divine plan. The process is not always a smooth one. Clarity will return and with it, freedom.

Dear World

28th November

There are always different paths to follow through the forest that may lead to hidden gems. Well-worn paths provide a familiar and ritualistic pattern to settle the mind and spirit, but the joy of exploration and discovery is a tonic to the soul, when other means of fun are few and far between. There is also a way in which the discovery of new outer paths stimulates new neural pathways within.

Dear World

29th November

It has come to our attention that not all is well in your world. That is a sadness to us and our representatives on earth. We are endeavouring to improve the situation. There is much to be said about the lack of empathy among some of your earth people that is causing trouble for many, but this has for a long time been so. We would hope that at these times they would understand the need for a communal approach. Frustration leads to rash behaviour it is true, but it is not too much to ask that you take care of one another and the planet. That is our wish and desire.

Dear World

30th November

There is a beauty and companionship in the telling of a good story around a winter's fire. Words can transport children and adult alike to different times and worlds where everyday rules can be suspended a little. The supernatural world of faery, elf and giant is familiar even to children and teaches much about archetypal energies within and without. Bring a little of the forest into the home, light a few candles and share a story or two. In doing so you connect with a stream of wisdom, love and tradition that lives beyond the fashions and trappings of any one era.

Dear World

1ˢᵗ December

It has been said that there are many ways to crack a nut and this is true of course. The squirrel, however, saves his for another day by storing in the ground and although he may not find them all, those that he does not, may grow into trees and continue to produce an ongoing harvest in future years. The moral of this then is that not all endeavours bring immediate harvests. Some bear fruit in the future, not always for self, but for the benefit of others. This is the way of life, sustainability in action.

Dear World

2nd December

Let us try to understand the means at your disposal to do this better. The anxiety ridden society that has been created as a result of this year and the ones before, is malfunctioning in many ways. There is an atmosphere of fear that is used to encourage required action. It is not always intended, but prevails, nonetheless. Action through love is always the better way. Consider your actions or non-action and how that may or may not cause harm to others. This is a good motivation to start and will lead naturally to what action or non-action is best carried out to bring things into a better way of being. It sounds simple and in many ways that is so, but often the simple actions and truths are forgotten in the need to over complicate things. Simple good intent, if well meant, is the key.

Dear World

3rd December

There is a fine line between devotion and obsession. It has been the dilemma within religions for centuries. Inflexibility of mind leads to inflexibility of body and where institutions are involved, they also may become too rigid. Connection and intercession between the normal, everyday earthly world and the spiritual world is never meant to be to the exclusion of the other. As has been said many times, lives need to be lived in order to grow in spirit. Relationship with and appreciation of the spiritual level in self and beyond is beneficial to self and in bringing that awareness to others. However, we do not encourage this above and beyond care of fellow humanity and other earthly life.

Dear World

4th December

Beneath the feet there is a movement and a stirring. Let sleeping dogs lay, they say, but what of the dragons that live below. Their breath is stirring with a glowing warmth that hints of the fire within. They are the guardians of land, sea and air and care little for the subtleties of life. When the earth stirs, the dragons stir. When the root of humanity is stirred, the dragons awake. A story yet to be told is forming in the ether. What is done is done. The future is becoming in the present. The taming of man and beast is not enslavement.

Dear World

5th December

An everchanging world exists before you. Showers of light fall down upon you all, landing on some like flakes of snow, others lay a moment on the earth then sink below. In this way, tree, mountain, fox, badger and all that lies below are being blessed. The tears of man and god are never wasted. The earth mother washes the wounds of life clean. The shining one awaits the call and all is known to all.

Dear World

6th December

Within the soul of man there are many chambers. In that we mean chambers of existence or reality. It is as if, in your soul there are cathedrals, caverns and temples of great sacredness and splendour, for if they do not exist within you, they cannot exist without. In these inner temples there is a continuous song that calls to and heals the fractured soul. A thousand choirs within ring out to the one vibration.

Dear World

7th December

In a multi-coloured world what hue are you. An uncomfortable society seeks to define by what means it can, for that which is undefinable is a threat to the status quo and rule of law, as they see it. You have taken many forms in your existence. Even in a lifetime you may live many chapters. Whether you look at a single lifetime or a multitude, it is this multiplicity of experience, whether through your own experience or that of others, that gives insight and understanding of others. You have all been many colours, worn many shoes and sometimes none.

Dear World

8th December
There is always another bridge to cross, another path to walk, or hill to climb. The passage of the year is long and not quite over. Not yet time to rest or leave this one behind. One last push towards the solstice and then new doors begin to open.

Dear World

9th December

It is said that you should always look forward and not dwell on the past. It is true that it pays little dividend to look too nostalgically or forlornly at the past, but the past as you see it is always informing the present and future. That is why, as people look towards a different possibility ahead, they are at the same time re-evaluating the past. What seemed acceptable to you a few decades ago may be no longer so and this is also true of the collective past. It is often a matter of focus. Those 'achievements' which were celebrated still exist, but the modern sensitivity may also be more discerning of other costs and social consequence. This is how it should be. Each time has its focus and viewpoint. Some degree of compassion and detachment helps if you are not to feel overwhelmed by anger or hurt about past realisations.

Dear World

10th December

So here you all are near a year's end, looking back at what you have and have not done. Always a time to take stock and count your blessings. There is a depth of feeling that can penetrate the being, brought about by Christmas times remembered and the wider remembrance that that provokes. For most at least these are happy and fond memories and bring an inner smile. There may be some regret at that which is lost, but always some determination to carry that joy forward. This is the tradition that passes from generation to generation and has from many ages past been so.

Dear World

11th December

It is within the capacity of your understanding to grasp what has been written here. There are many words, but there meaning is fathomable if cryptic at times. There is a way in which the words flow, sometimes easier than others, depending on the subject and direction of their source. It is never about absolute truths, but interpretation of the world, its energy systems and spiritual influences. Consciousness is a choice, but so is ignorance. Knowledge is sometimes uncomfortable, but if it deepens our understanding then it will ultimately be of benefit to self and others.

Dear World

12th December

The eyes of a child see so much more than the eyes of an adult. They see a dream that gave birth to what now exists. They see the reality of right and wrong, stripped bare of the attachments of worrying about what others think. They see wonder in nature, a leaf, flower, puddle or twig. It is not too late to regain the eyes of a child. As the days shorten the child within awakens. An annual remembrance awaits.

Dear World

13th December

The road of no consequence is easy to follow. Those that do, realise no comeback for their actions and attitudes, because there are none of any great influence. It takes some courage to follow a path of consequence. The healer, mystic, poet and magician take hold of the reins of influence and steer towards the light of truth and knowledge. The consequences of failure are very real to those that try and also to the theatre of influence in which they operate, but the consequences of avoidance are far greater for all. A troubled world is in need of the way-showers and risk-takers. In this, new worlds are born.

Dear World

14th December

You lay down upon your bed, but rest does not always come to you. The whirling's of the mind and passions of the heart are stirring. Sometimes you know not where these feelings come from. The fire in the head ignites thoughts and words. Fire in the belly drives action if you are able to take it and fire in the heart seeks passion of ideals or relationship. It may be that the denial of freedoms lights the spark, or is it the movements of the stars and heavens above.

Dear World

15th December

There will always be some who do not believe. They do not believe in science or they do not believe in god. Others do not believe in fairies or spiritual dimensions and beings. When you dig below the surface there is always something in which they do believe, whether it is unique to themselves or created by the mind of another, matters not. It shows that they have the imaginative faculties to believe in something, often unprovable. Most of you can rationalise your beliefs to some extent, but at some point you have to admit that in part you have to take it on faith.

Your experience and knowing encourages you to believe and if you share some of your beliefs with others, they are re-enforced. Revelation and experience shapes the beliefs of individuals, communities and nations and it is not for us to judge, if they do no harm, but this process is ongoing, so remember to refresh your outlook and encourage others to do the same. It is prudent to do so in a fast changing, dynamic world and time-space.

Dear World

16th December

Wherever you go I will be. I am the one who stands behind you when you wobble. I am the calm within a storm, the food that sustains your hunger and the rain that makes your garden grow. I am the tears that wash your pain away, the song that speaks to your heart. I am the baby that has total faith in you and the fruit amongst the thorns.

Dear World

17th December

You stress and you worry about what is to come. You feel like time is slipping through your hands and nothing can be done. Do not worry, there is time a plenty to do what needs to be done. Accept what is the now, for that is all there is in this moment. Tomorrow is another day and it will be revealed in its own good time. Not everything has to be done at once. Breathe a little, you are doing ok. Remember what life is teaching you. We are all in this together and will emerge when the unfolding begins.

Dear World

18th December

It is always a question on your mind; am I worthy of being loved? All beings are worthy of being loved for they are born of love. Acceptance and love go hand in hand, acceptance of who we are and loving ourselves for that. It is also our fulfilment to love other beings for what they are. It is not for everyone to be the same. You can disapprove of certain actions, but this does not deter from the precipitators need for existence. None are perfect in this state. When you can attain these moments of recognition for the beauty and love for all existence, there is a release and completeness in yourself that is at one with that completed circle of love.

Dear World

19th December

All are one in this respect, that is all are dealing with the same enemy, as it were. The ability to encourage adaptability in humanity is challenged by the adaptability of the disease you are facing. These are extraordinary times of course. Never before, has the rapidity of outward change been such a challenge to the adaptability of all organisms on earth. The smallest organisms adapt the fastest and this has always been a stimulator of evolution in other life forms. We are not encouraging a placid outlook in this respect, but an observation of events may encourage learning and more speedy resolution. The group mind is at work from both sides of the playing field. It may be that this is the level at which to begin healing of the situation.

Dear World

20th December

There is light at the end of the tunnel. Nowhere is oblivious to the light that shines from above. The silver moon shines upon the midnight forests that await the return of the winter sun. The stillness of fresh fallen snow is ready to absorb the silent footsteps of those abroad at this longest of nights.

Dear World

21ˢᵗ December

It has always been so that we celebrate the returning sun. The familiarity to your soul and peer group is plain to see. Celebration can come in many ways though. It is appropriate for some to be loud and exuberant in their joyful shenanigans, but it is also as effective to quietly open to the energy and sacred nature of the season. Eating something in a spirit of sharing with those unseen as well as any present is appreciated. Take a little time to allow yourself to also give thanks for getting through the darkest night and enjoying the fruits of the season. Feel blessed, because you are.

Dear World

22nd December

They sleep beyond the veil awaiting rebirth, as the months and days turn onward. The time of renewal is upon you. Yes, take a pause, rejoice and rest a while. When the time is right their presence will be felt. In the meantime, do as you would do. Forever seeking the truth just out of reach is always commendable and fun if the endeavour is undertaken with a lightness of heart and mood. This is after all the season to be jolly is it not.

Dear World

23rd December

What is it that you seek? Is it peace and quiet? Or is it satisfaction in work and home life? There is a tendency in the western world to never be quite satisfied with what you have and wanting just that little bit more, whether that be in a material sense or in terms of spiritual gains and improved relationships with others. It is not without merit to strive forward in the service of fellow man and the wider world, but as always there is a balance to be struck. So many of you suffer with tension in body and mind, because you are feeling hemmed in while wanting to do much more. This physical manifestation of an inner state is very real, but only a limitation if you allow it to be so. The stillness that is to be found within the moment is a gift if you allow it to be so.

Dear World

24th December

There is in the eve of Christmas, a promise of things to come, stillness, candlelight and reverence for the holiness of tradition that it holds. There is in that anticipation sometimes more than in the day that follows. It was often the way in the past to hold ceremony and ritual on the night before a significant festival or event. Maybe it is all in the preparation, in the way in which you settle your mind, body and spirit for what is to follow. Give thanks for what you have and will give and receive and send thoughts and prayers to those who will not be so fortunate. Whatever you believe, Christmas is a culturally and symbolically important day of the year and to many it is much more.

Dear World

25th December

The big day comes and goes with a plethora of traditions and memories half-forgotten beneath the surface. You have satisfied what has always been done and that seems to have fulfilled an ancient contract, but somewhere behind it all there is a hollowness that maybe ponders a question. Do not worry too much about the fulfilment of duties at this time. You have celebrated with a good heart and awareness of those less fortunate. You have celebrated your gifts and blessings in the promise of what is to follow. This is an important undertaking and is all that is required at this time.

Dear World

26th December

There is a peace in these few days following Christmas when the mad rush has died down and most are still not at their work. The time is ripe for indulgence in a little of what you fancy; from a good long walk, engaging in some craft or other interest, to just relaxing at home. It is a time that allows us to reconsider and re-align our sleepy souls to the new year soon to follow.

Dear World

27th December

As we tidy away loose ends, clear space and make way for the new, we are left wondering what was all that for. Do not focus on the difficulties and stresses that the last year brought, but on the benefits. Consider the deepening of your relationship with yourself. Do you not know yourself a little better? You know what you are willing to go without and that which you are not. You are also more aware of that which you can and cannot tolerate. The acquiring of this knowledge may have been painful, but its benefits will be ongoing. That which you seek now lies before you and you are better equipped to seek it out and to know what is fool's gold. In this way no experience is ever wasted.

Dear World

28th December

Between the worlds we stand awaiting news from those that have gone ahead. Surely, they must have found a gap in the fence, a chink in the armour to give us hope and restoration. There is a way in which the future we seek already exists within us. It is just for us to feel that within ourselves and give it energy. In this way new worlds are created.

Dear World

29th December

Total surrender is sometimes all that is left. If you find yourself in a safe place, but are not sure how to deal with outside events or the road ahead, then surrender yourself as you sit in meditation or contemplation. Surrender to a state of acceptance to what has befallen and the current situation. Everything happens for a reason they say and there is much truth in this. Breathe with it and allow the possibility of magic to enter into your life and life as a whole. Let doorways open and synchronicity to find you. In this state of grace there is much to be thankful for.

Dear World

30th December

So, you all have emotions, feelings and desires, even you spiritual ones, in fact even more so. It may be that at times on your path that you find the need to deny or override these feelings in order to focus on the whole. Although this is at times desirable and necessary for your growth, it is not ultimately the divine consequence. Ultimately the central pulse in the universe is love and therefore it is foolhardy in the end to block the flow. The stream finds its way to the river and the river flows to the sea. The water within you will find its way home.

Dear World

31st December

It has been a long and troubled year for most, but not without its revelations. To look back at its treasured moments is a good practice to observe. Many words have been given to you, all in good faith and hope of understanding. As is often the case, their worth may not become apparent until time has passed. None the matter, it is enough that the seed of their truth has entered your consciousness and this will spawn new ideas and openings. Be good to yourselves on this night, you have walked your path well and are looking forward to the year to come.

Acknowledgments

Firstly, I must give thanks to those who guide me in the spiritual realms, without whom this book would not exist. I also thank my mum for giving me the shining example of resilience through pain and difficult circumstances and my dad for teaching me the observance and appreciation of nature. These gifts have greatly influenced the completion of this book. I would also like to mention my dear friend, natural medium, spiritual teacher and artist Bonnie Roud for reminding me of my spiritual connection when I wander from it. I held close in heart and mind my circles of spiritual and magical friends when meditating for this book, with their connection I am blessed. I would particularly like to thank all those who followed my Dear World Facebook page, giving me encouragement to continue with these daily inspirations. My gratitude to the Order of Bards, Ovates and Druids can also not be underestimated for giving a home to my spiritual path for the last twenty-five years that suits my questing soul. Last and not least I give love and thanks to my wider family for keeping me grounded, loved and supported during this most trying of years.